HUMAN-POWERED POETRY from the APPALACHIAN TRAIL

A Thru-hiker's Perspective

Daniel "Screech" Zube

GEORGIA TO MAINE

MAY 1 – SEPTEMBER 18, 2017

Peter E. Randall Publisher
Portsmouth, NH
2019

 First published 2019
ISBN: 978-1-937721-77-0
Library of Congress Control Number: 2018963269
Published by
Peter E. Randall Publisher
Box 4726
Portsmouth, NH 03802
www.perpublisher.com
Book design by: Tim Holtz

AUTHOR'S PREFACE

Explore the outdoors
Unplug from our modern world
Connect with nature

They say the Appalachian Trail transforms the people who hike it – physically, mentally, psychologically – you name it. I'll be honest, I thought I knew myself quite well at thirty-four years of age, so I quickly dismissed this notion and figured it did not apply to me. Thankfully, I was wrong.

Early in 2017, I received a surprising invitation from a very generous friend to spend the month of March rafting 280 miles of the Colorado River through Grand Canyon National Park (GCNP) in Arizona. I had been living in Colorado for the past nine years, and though I always thought I would eventually return to New England, where I grew up, I never knew when. If a rafting trip through GCNP was not the right way to conclude my time out west and head back east, then I knew the right time would never come. So, I bid farewell to an amazing community of friends in Colorado and set off into the remote desert wilderness carrying armfuls of borrowed river gear and the following haiku written by my mother on a small piece of paper:

Grand Canyon delight
Adventures around each bend
Rafting on a dream

On the very last night of the rafting trip, I removed this piece of paper from one of my dry bags to recall the syllable pattern of a haiku and wrote my first one. Up to this point in my life, I had never written a single poem, but I thought the exercise might help me stay awake during the "night float" along the calm, flat, forty-mile section of river before the take-out at Pearce Ferry. More haikus followed as the hours and miles slowly trickled by while witnessing the moonrise, moonset, and gradual emergence of the Milky Way. The creative energy needed to generate these simple haikus enabled me to keep watch over the river and occasionally shout "*BUUUUUMP!*" to warn the fifteen sleeping crewmembers of an impending collision with the canyon wall. I wrote until the sounds of bats and crickets were replaced by birdsong, and the silhouettes of towering cliffs slowly revealed their features to daylight. This experience introduced me to a newfound ability to leverage mindfulness as a vehicle for entertainment amidst the silence and solitude of wilderness.

Returning back to "reality" from such an epic adventure is like beginning to wake up from a dream you wish would never end. Logical thoughts of consciousness start to interfere with a fantasy world that is slipping away no matter how hard you close your eyes and pretend to be asleep. Reemergence is inevitable, but sometimes if you're lucky, it can be delayed. In this same vein, I was not yet ready to move across the country, establish a new community of friends, or find a new job and a new place to live. I yearned to return to the simplicity and peacefulness of nature, and I realized it was time to let go of expectations that were not my own and to drift into another dream on the Appalachian Trail (AT).

In Georgia, at the outset of my thru-hike, I realized that despite being in a dramatically different climate zone than Arizona, these two special places in the American landscape share the same wilderness. I was thankful to be surrounded by nature once again, but hiking alone through a forest on a clearly marked trail requires noticeably less mental focus than navigating through death-defying white-water rapids. If I planned to walk 2189.8 miles to Maine, I knew I would have to entertain myself along the way. I considered listening to music or podcasts but was curious to see how long I could go without, and I never ended up needing them. Instead, I focused my attention on the surrounding landscapes, critters, people, and places encountered along the AT, and I reflected on these observations to ward off boredom in the same way I had done during the night float to Pearce Ferry.

Expressing these thoughts through poetry was not only entertaining, but it also provided a means of capturing the AT experience in real time, much like a journal. I achieved this by speaking into my smartphone while I was hiking and utilizing the voice-to-text feature to record the poems without stopping. In fact, the only way I found it possible to formulate poems was by physically being in the act of hiking, hence, "human-powered poetry." I tried to write poems at night before bed, in the morning during breakfast, or even during the day when I would stop and rest, but I couldn't do it – I had to be moving. The rhythm of my footsteps generated these poems through a process which then motivated me to continue hiking onward to Katahdin as a poetry-powered human.

After waking up from any memorable dream, you typically want to share it with someone right away before the details fade away. Unfortunately, no matter how good of a storyteller you are, it's just not the same as experiencing it for yourself. With this in mind, I hope the poems and photos contained in this book will inspire you to get outside, go on an adventure, and create your own experience.

Morning light so soft
We invite you to wake us
When the time is right

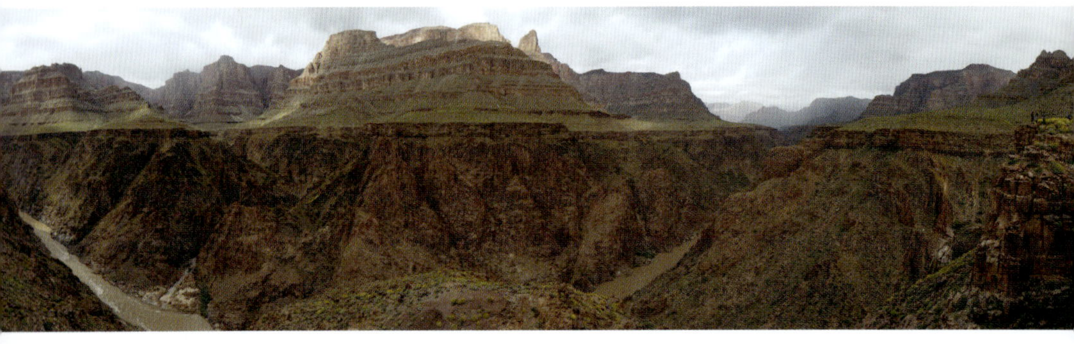

Thank you to all of my family, friends, trail magicians, and volunteers who supported me before, during, and after this adventure. You are the humans who power me.

—Daniel "Screech" Zube

HUMAN-POWERED POETRY from the APPALACHIAN TRAIL

A Thru-hiker's Perspective

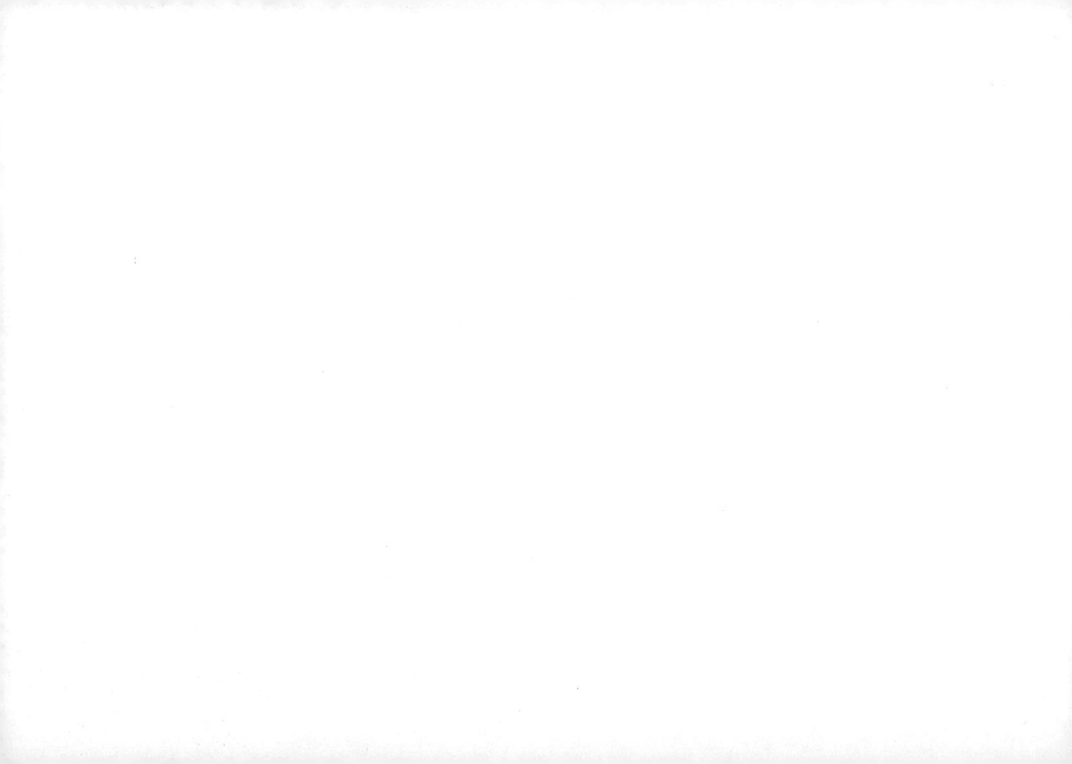

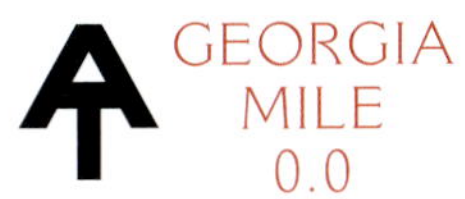

Betting today's time
On a better tomorrow
Is a tough wager

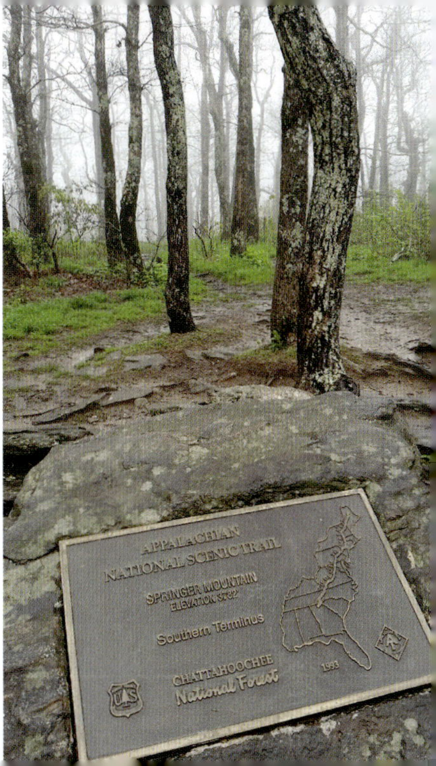

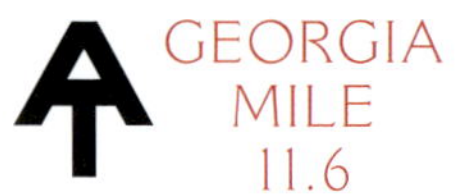

Running "ultralight"
Butterfly on my backpack
No free rides for you

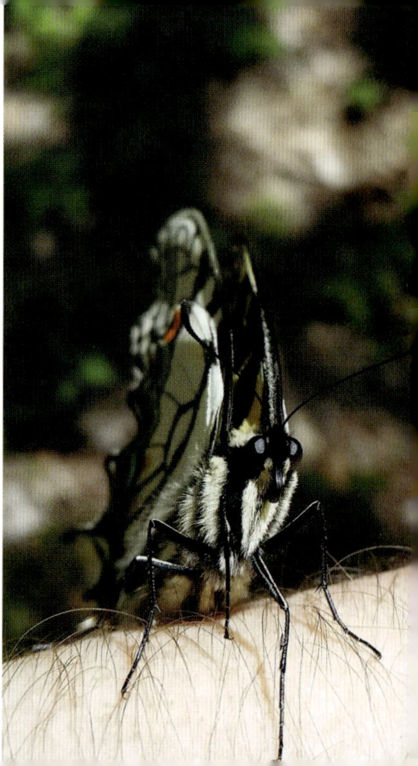

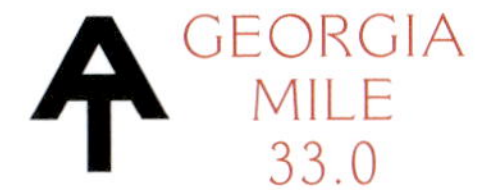

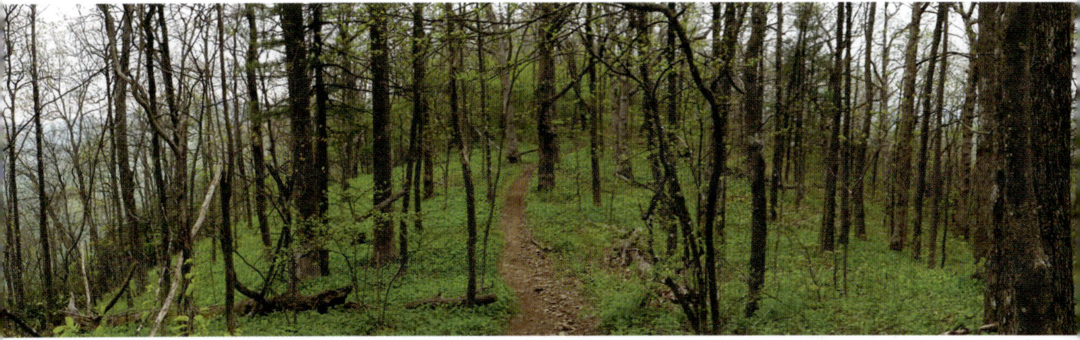

Wave of wind coming
Heard through forest canopy
Wait for it … here now

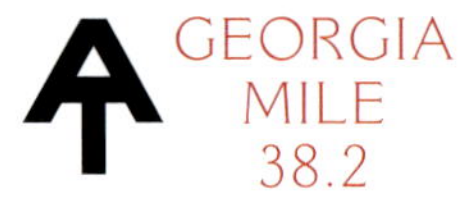

GEORGIA MILE 38.2

Hiking through a cloud
Peek-a-boo mountain-top view
Trails through mist vanish

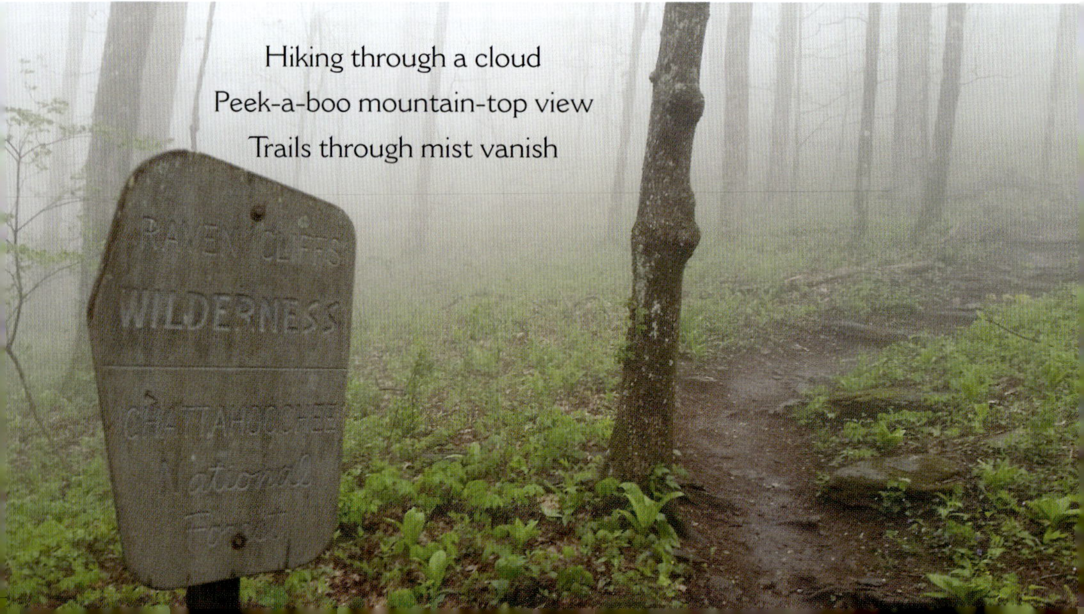

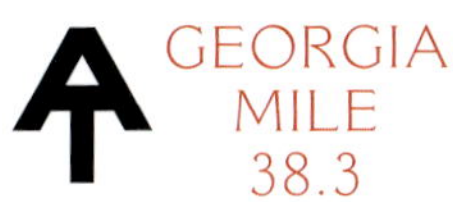

Droplet on my brow
Rain or sweat, what could it be?
Up Tesnatee Gap

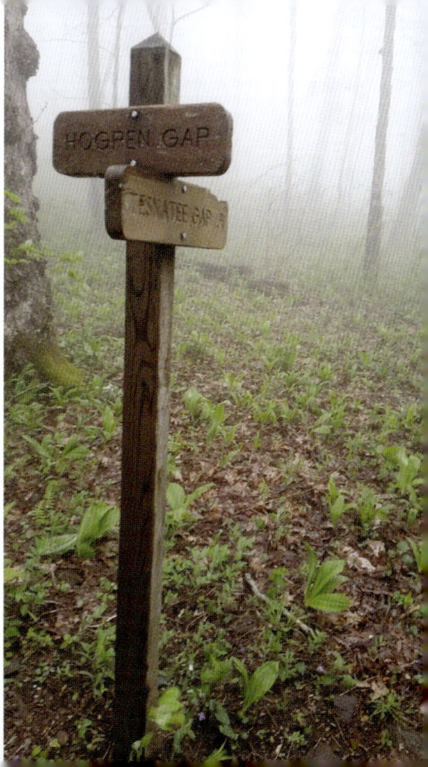

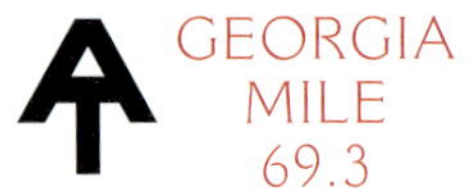

Backpackers' time warp
One week ago seems like months
Reference frame reset

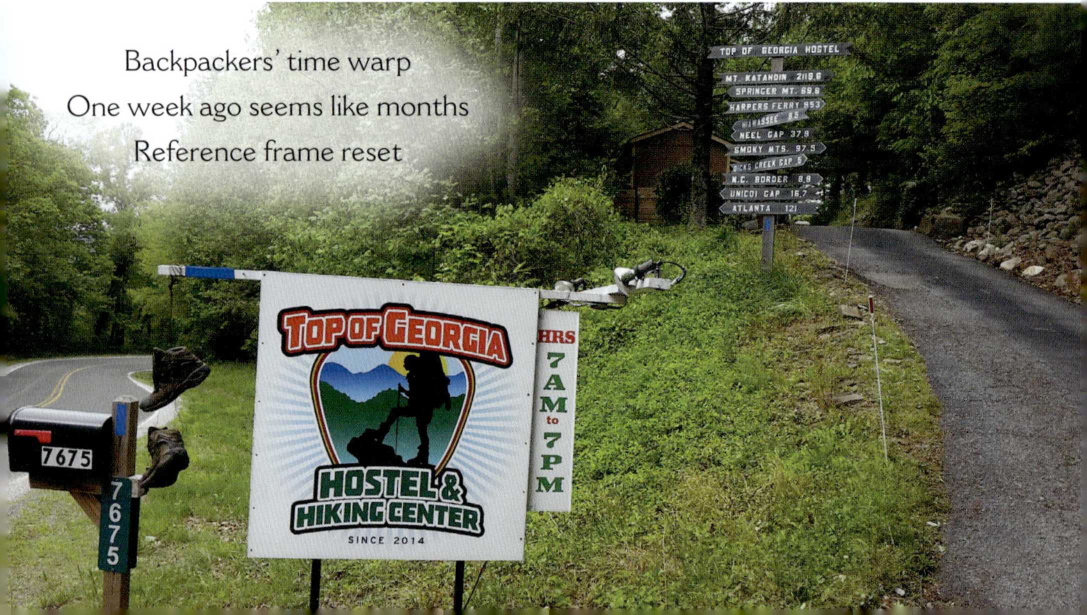

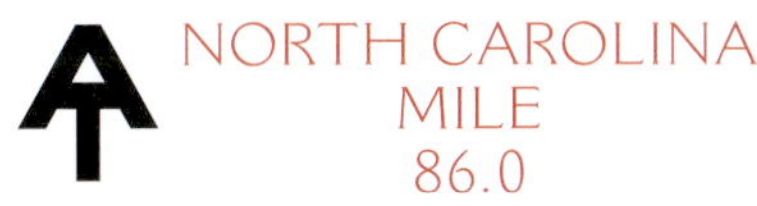

NORTH CAROLINA MILE 86.0

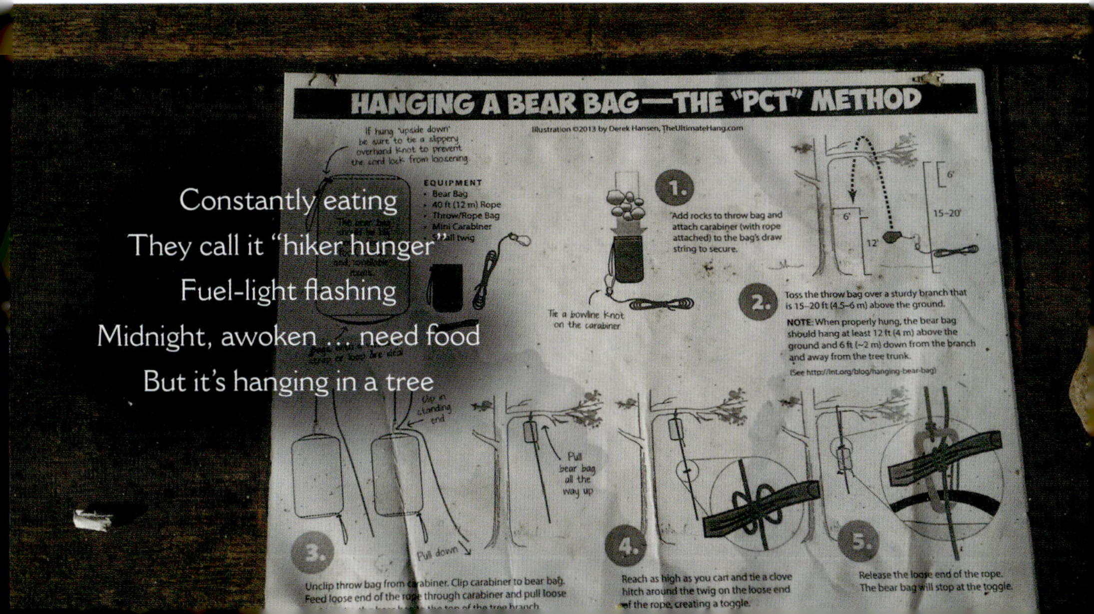

Constantly eating
They call it "hiker hunger"
Fuel-light flashing
Midnight, awoken … need food
But it's hanging in a tree

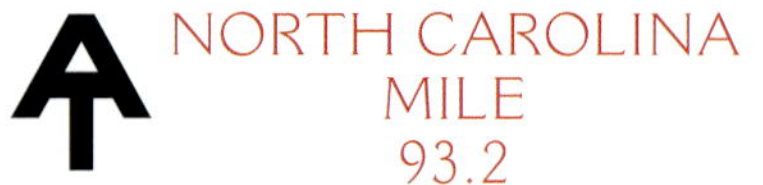

NORTH CAROLINA
MILE
93.2

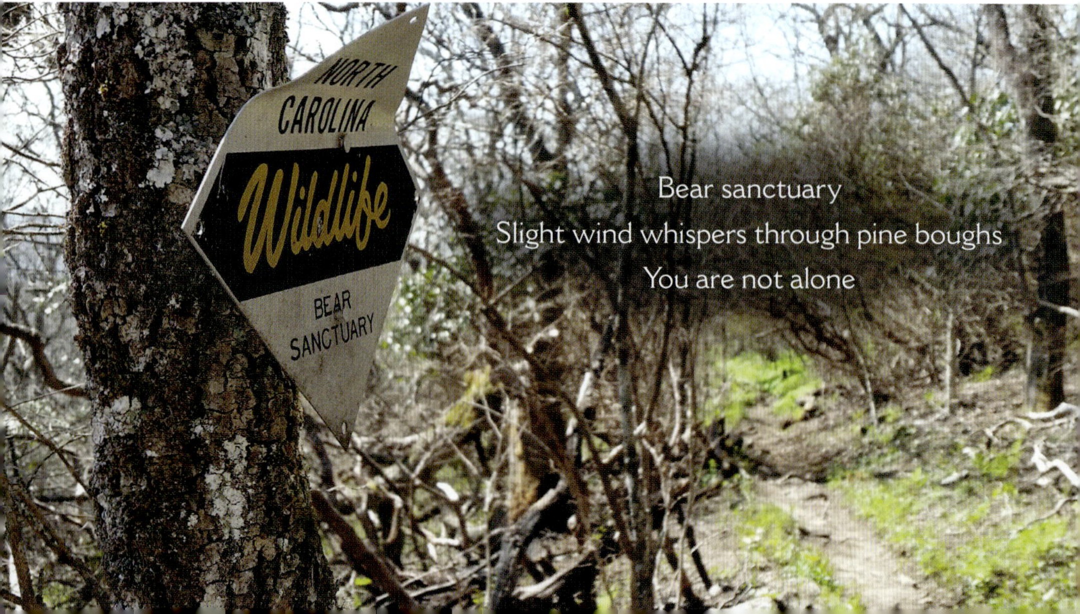

Bear sanctuary
Slight wind whispers through pine boughs
You are not alone

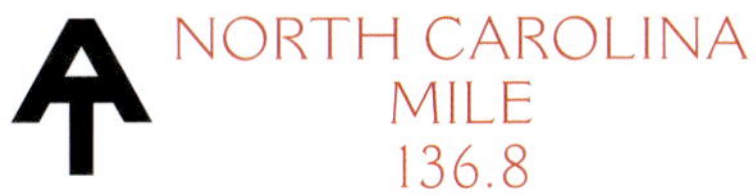

NORTH CAROLINA
MILE
136.8

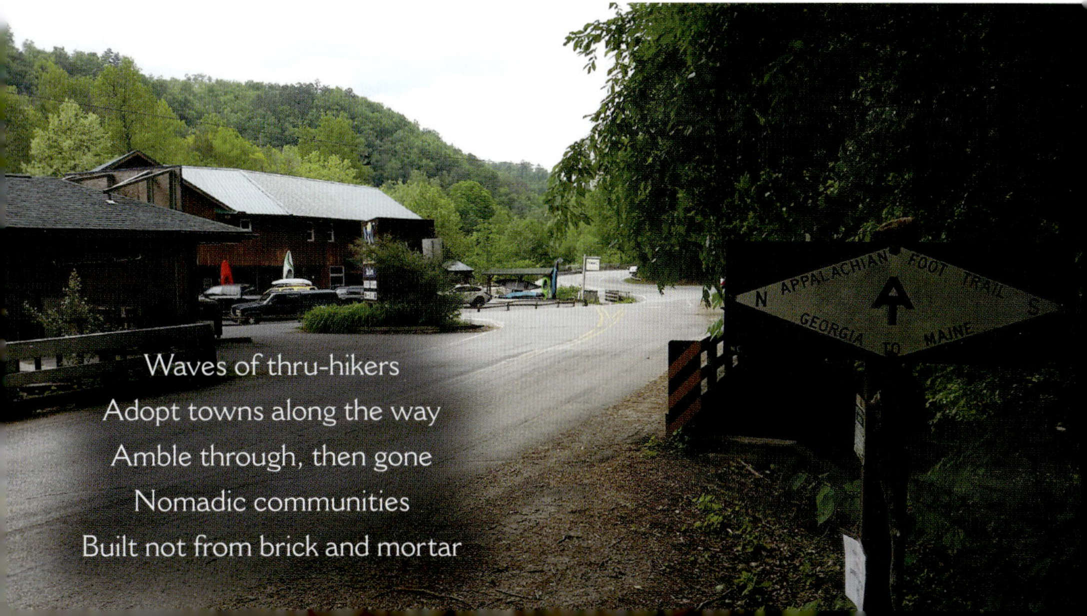

Waves of thru-hikers
Adopt towns along the way
Amble through, then gone
Nomadic communities
Built not from brick and mortar

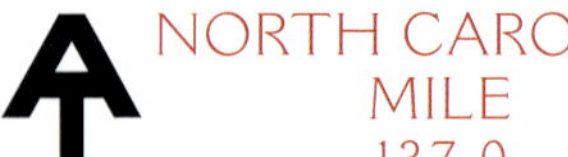

NORTH CAROLINA
MILE
137.0

Ziplock bags are a thru-hiker must
Beware of generics and choose ones you can trust
There's more than one size
To help organize
Trail mix and maps, even liquids like jelly
Oatmeal and Band-Aids, and stuff that's real smelly
When they're all empty, don't you dare trash'm
Rinse'm n dry'm, 'til next time just stash'm
After use one-oh-two
When they're no longer see-through
Perhaps then you may have to use tape to rehash'm

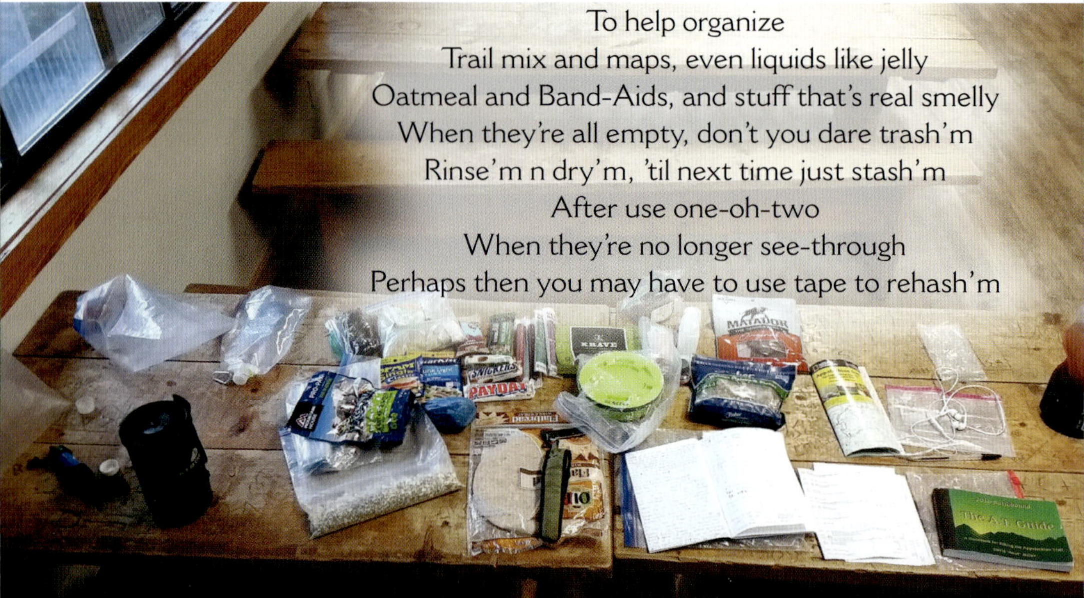

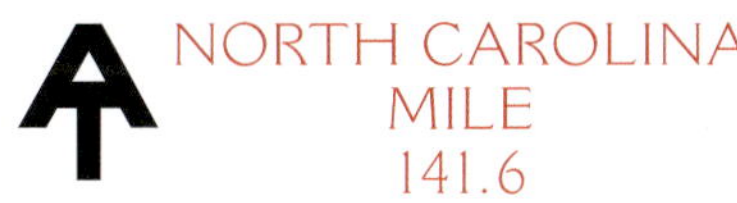

NORTH CAROLINA
MILE
141.6

Distracted hiker
Typing poems into phone
Smacks head on low branch

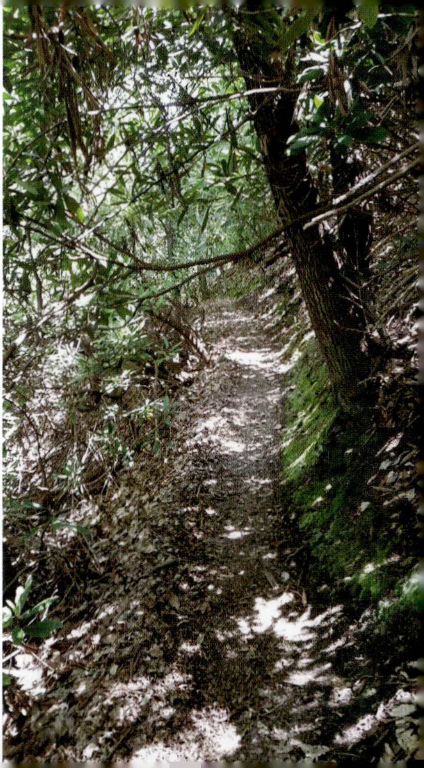

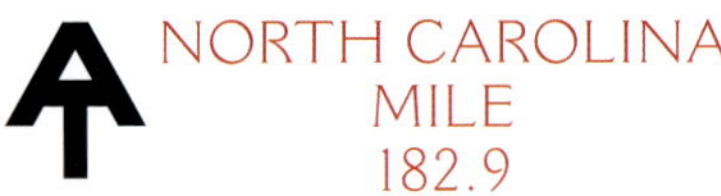

NORTH CAROLINA MILE 182.9

At the end of the day, when I fine-ly sit down
I'm promptly greeted by flies, swarming my crown
With no bug spray concoction
I have no other option
Than to put on my bug net and frown

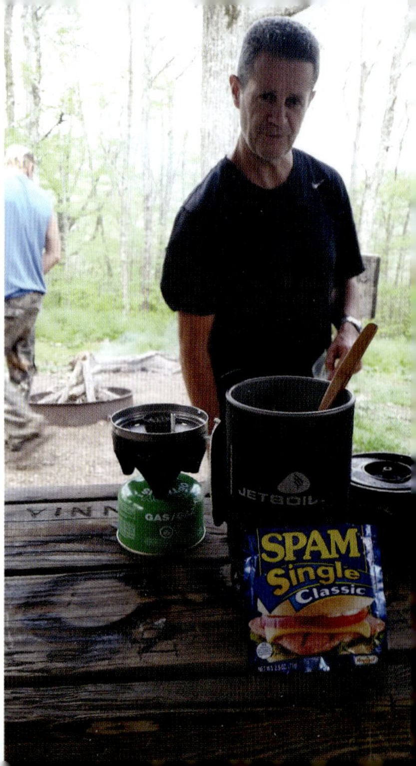

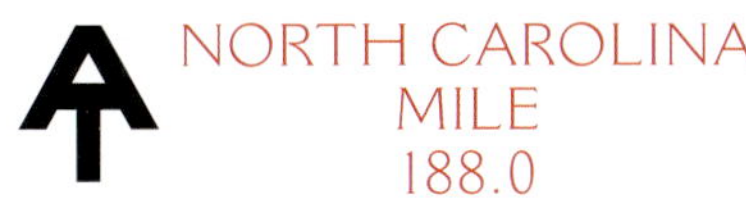

NORTH CAROLINA
MILE
188.0

Familiar faces
Fellow hikers on the move
All of us, northbound
Following the white blazes
Day to day, leapfrog we play

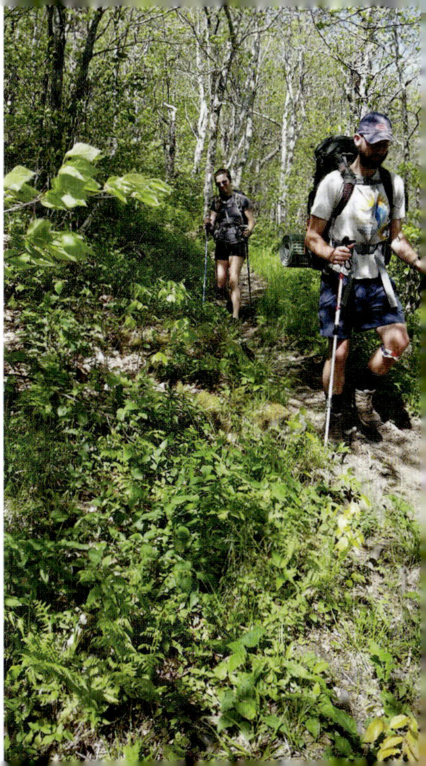

TENNESSEE
MILE
195.1

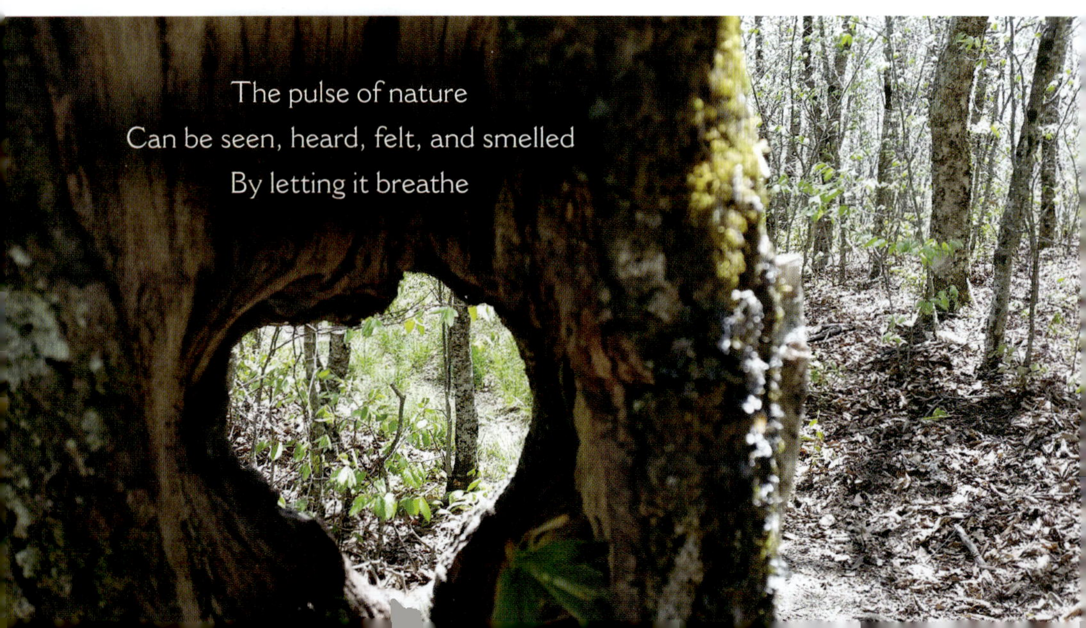

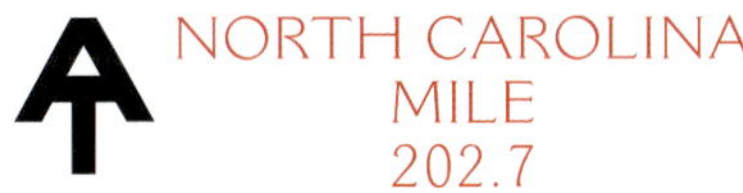

NORTH CAROLINA MILE 202.7

Forest transition
Deciduous yields to fir
Scent of Christmas trees
Dead trees wear sweaters of moss
AT ceiling within reach

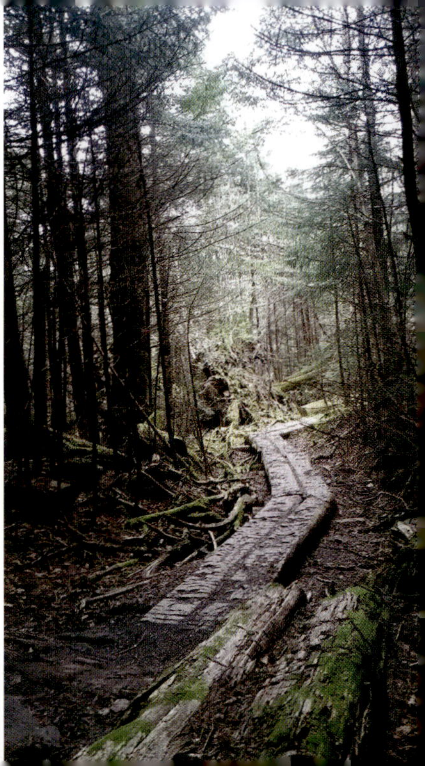

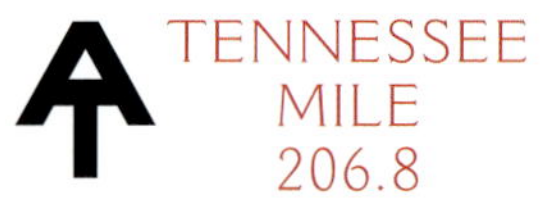

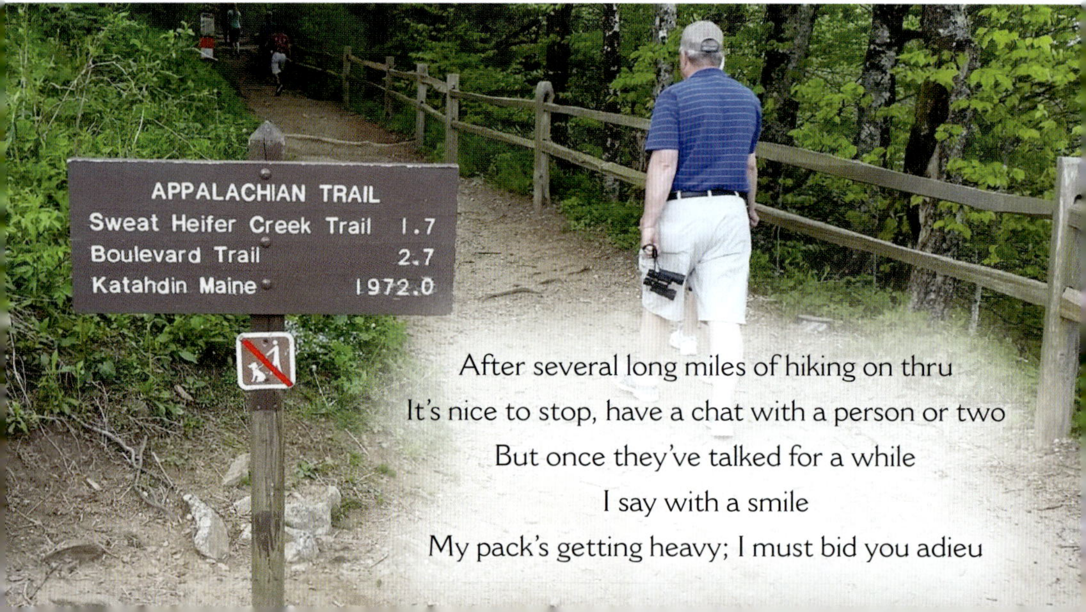

After several long miles of hiking on thru
It's nice to stop, have a chat with a person or two
But once they've talked for a while
I say with a smile
My pack's getting heavy; I must bid you adieu

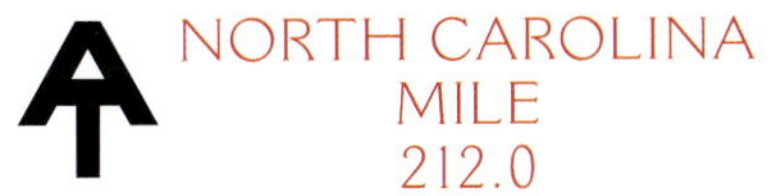

NORTH CAROLINA
MILE
212.0

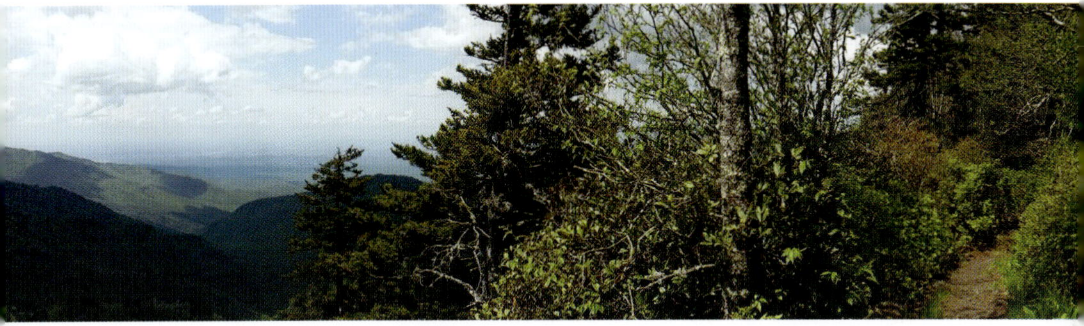

Left foot Tennessee
Right foot North Carolina
Ridge walker moves north
On a spine between two states
Great Smoky Mountains, they share

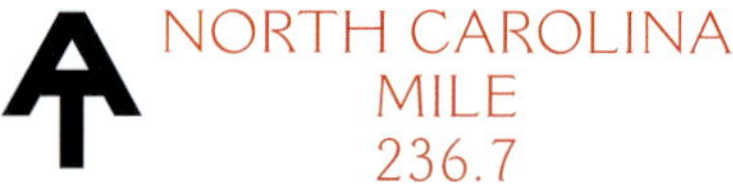

Mindfulness training
Moving to nature's rhythm
Five senses alert

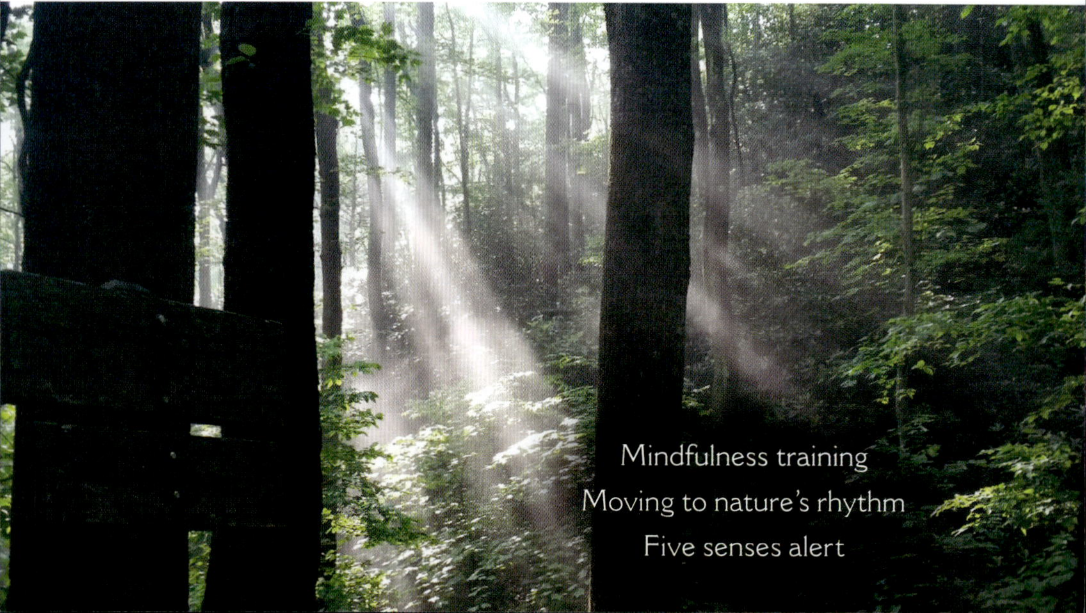

NORTH CAROLINA
MILE
239.5

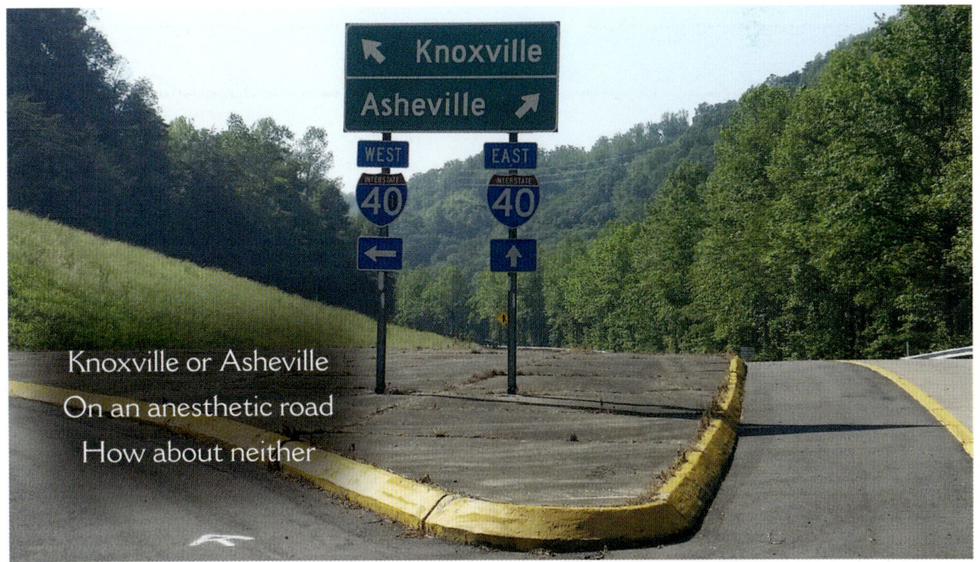

Knoxville or Asheville
On an anesthetic road
How about neither

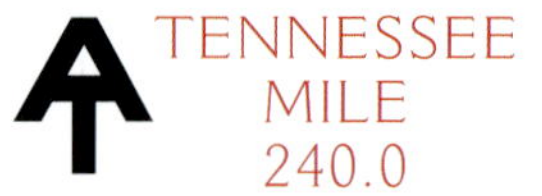

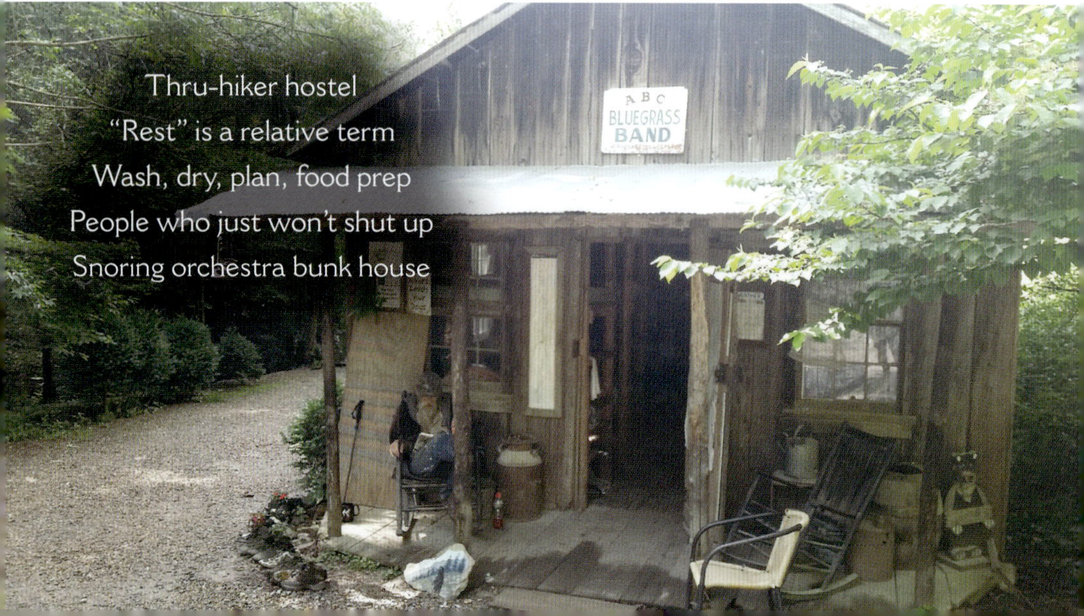

Thru-hiker hostel
"Rest" is a relative term
Wash, dry, plan, food prep
People who just won't shut up
Snoring orchestra bunk house

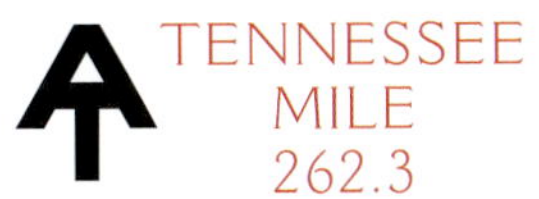

TENNESSEE MILE 262.3

Filtering water
16-minute walk away
Steep, bad trail, bugs bite
Three-point-five liters, twice … flow?
Makes pee seem like Niagara

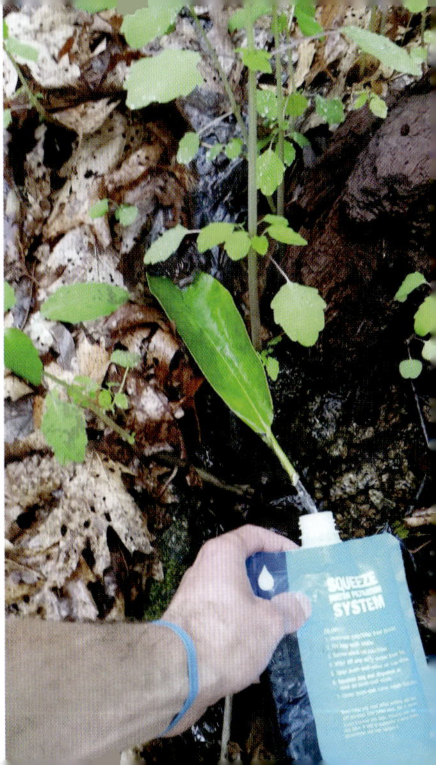

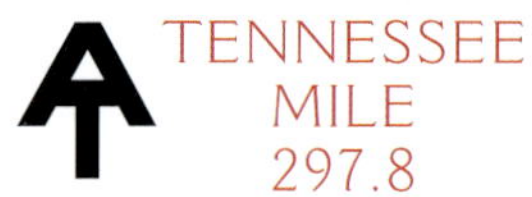

Spring unraveling
Flower petal confetti
Sprinkled before me
Thick canopies climb uphill
Last Fall's leaves turn to compost

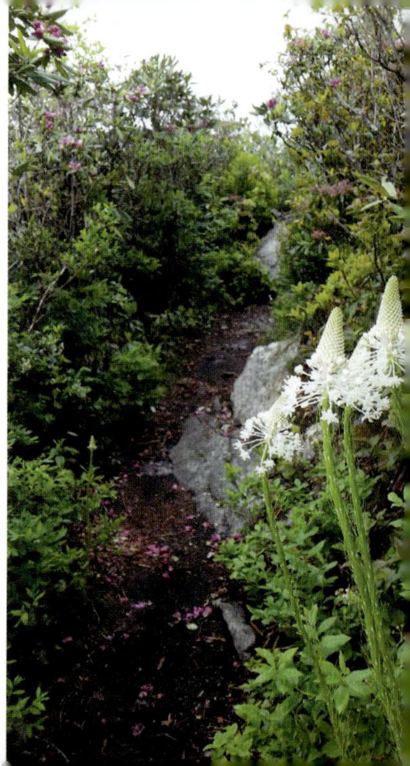

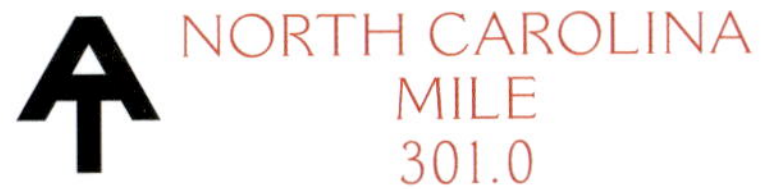

NORTH CAROLINA
MILE
301.0

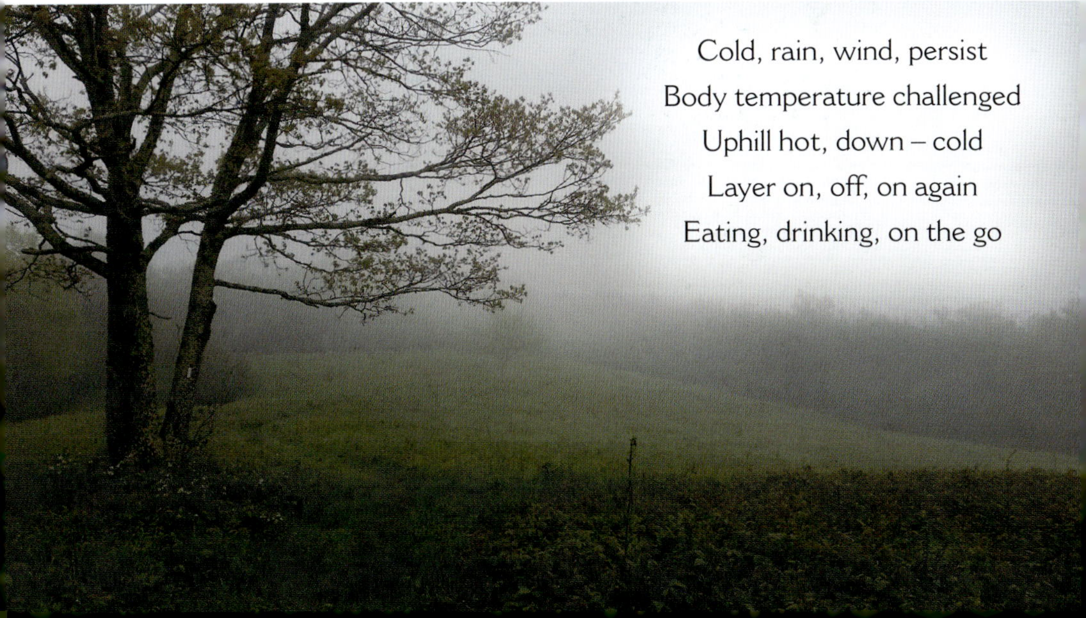

Cold, rain, wind, persist
Body temperature challenged
Uphill hot, down – cold
Layer on, off, on again
Eating, drinking, on the go

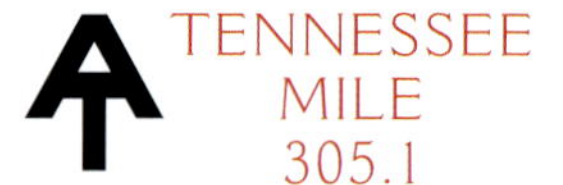

TENNESSEE
MILE
305.1

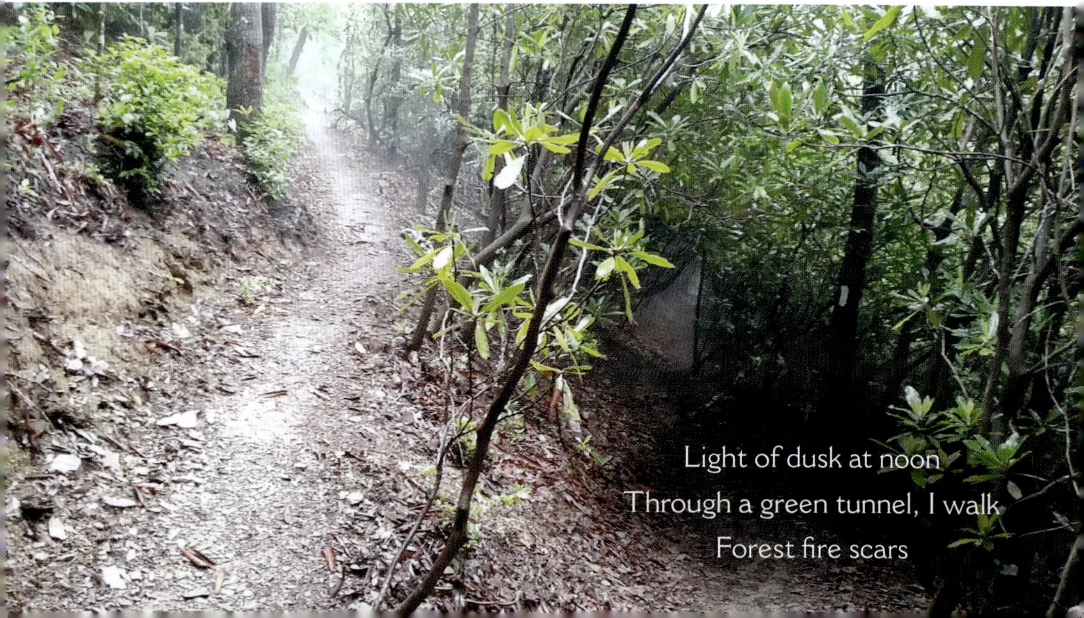

Light of dusk at noon
Through a green tunnel, I walk
Forest fire scars

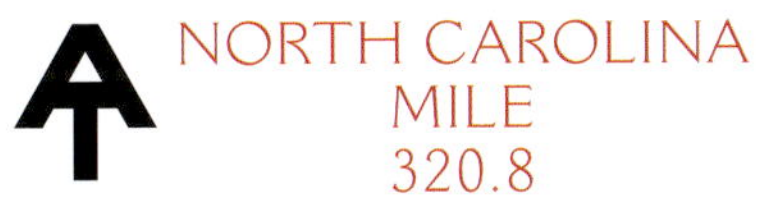

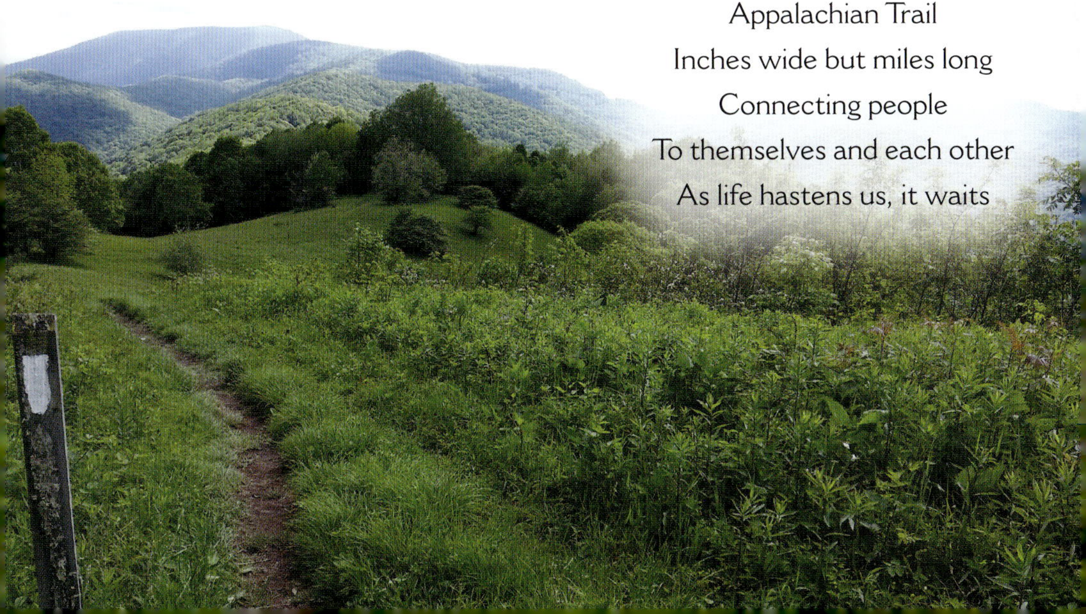

Appalachian Trail

Inches wide but miles long

Connecting people

To themselves and each other

As life hastens us, it waits

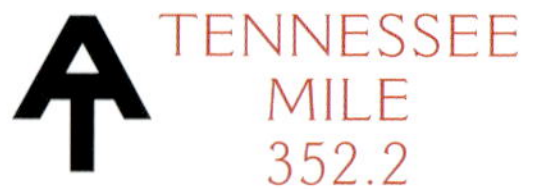

TENNESSEE
MILE
352.2

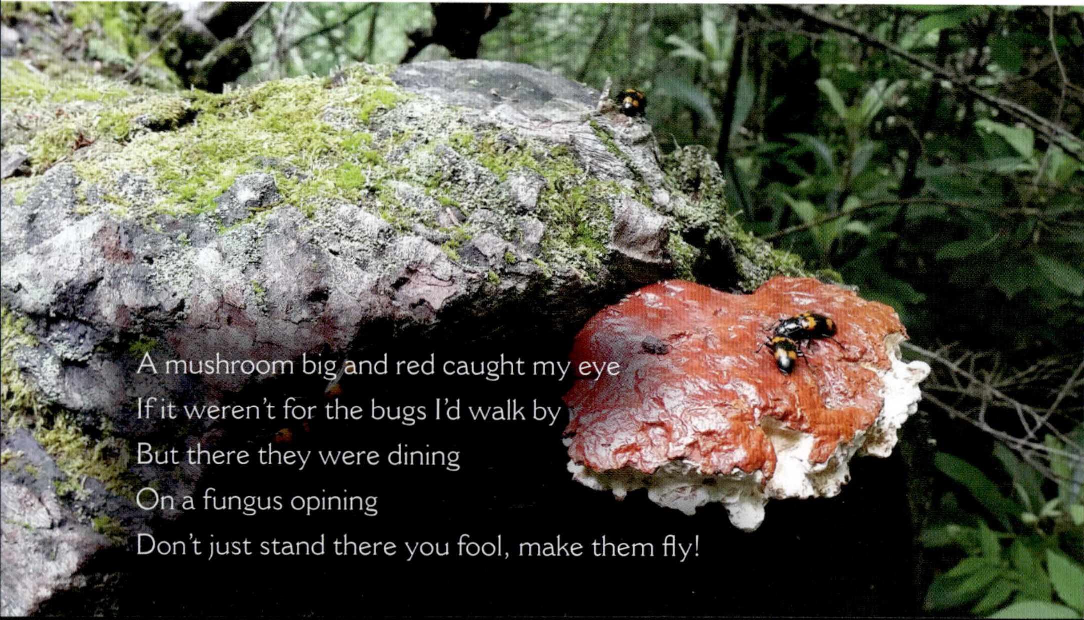

A mushroom big and red caught my eye
If it weren't for the bugs I'd walk by
But there they were dining
On a fungus opining
Don't just stand there you fool, make them fly!

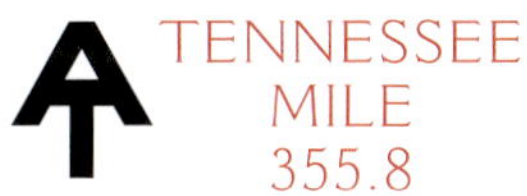

TENNESSEE MILE 355.8

Mountain laurel bloomed
Rhododendron nearly there
A race to nectar

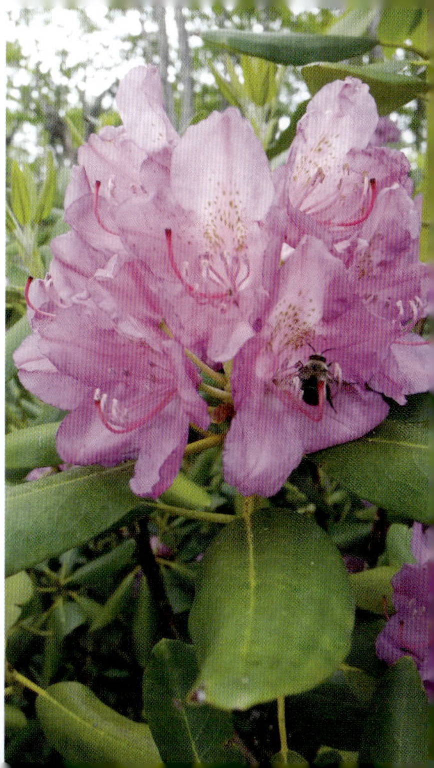

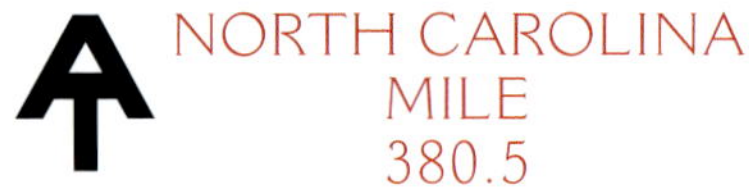

NORTH CAROLINA MILE 380.5

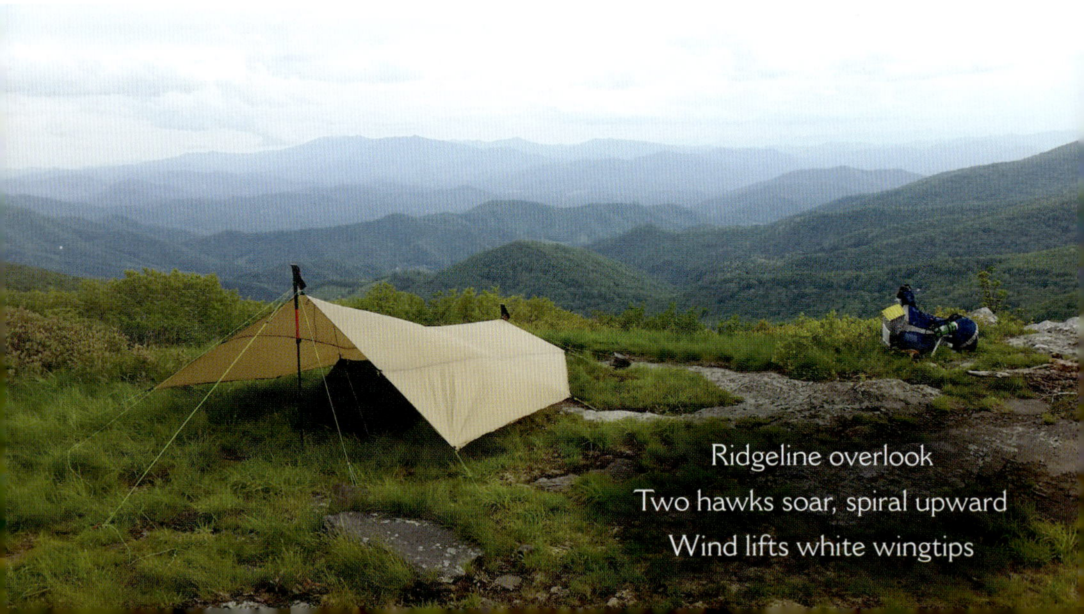

Ridgeline overlook
Two hawks soar, spiral upward
Wind lifts white wingtips

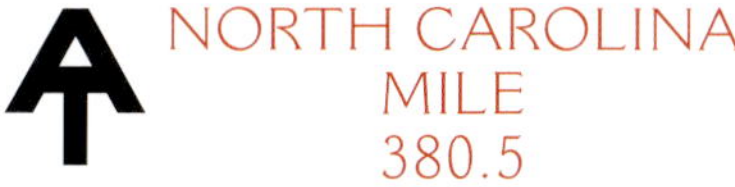

Fireflies play tricks
Glowing just for an instant
Weary eyes blinking
Staring out to unknown space
At everything and nothing
As a supine gaze
Searches for a shooting star
Imagining how
One may appear where I look
When the timing is just right

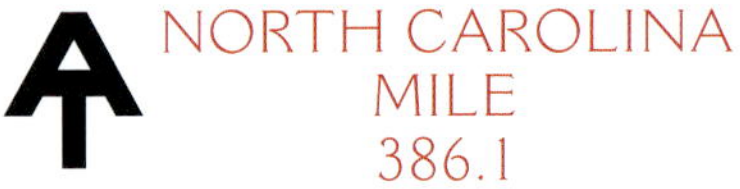

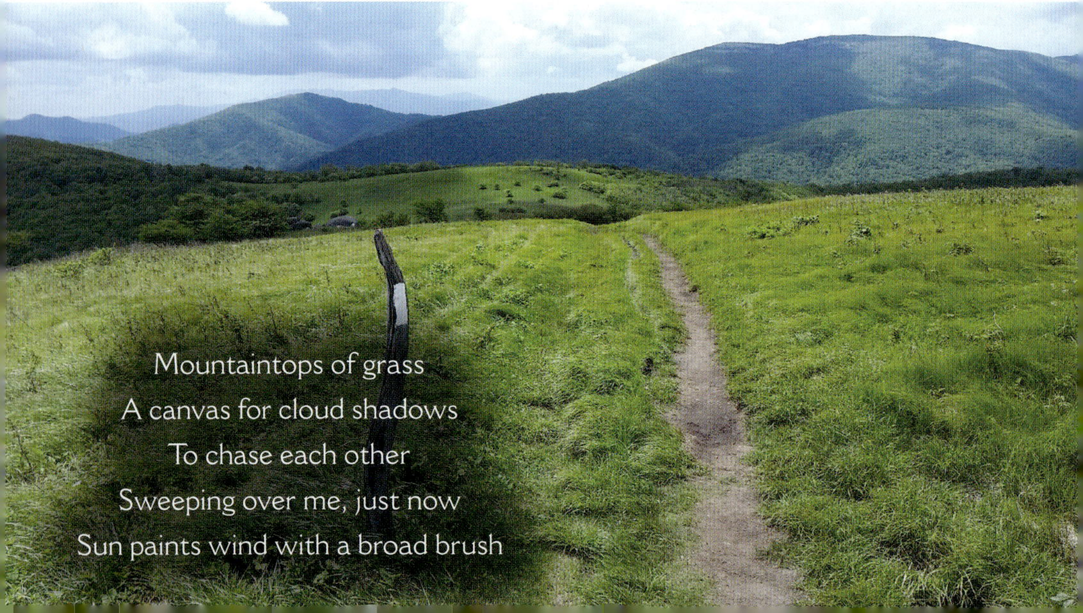

Mountaintops of grass
A canvas for cloud shadows
To chase each other
Sweeping over me, just now
Sun paints wind with a broad brush

TENNESSEE
MILE
400.5

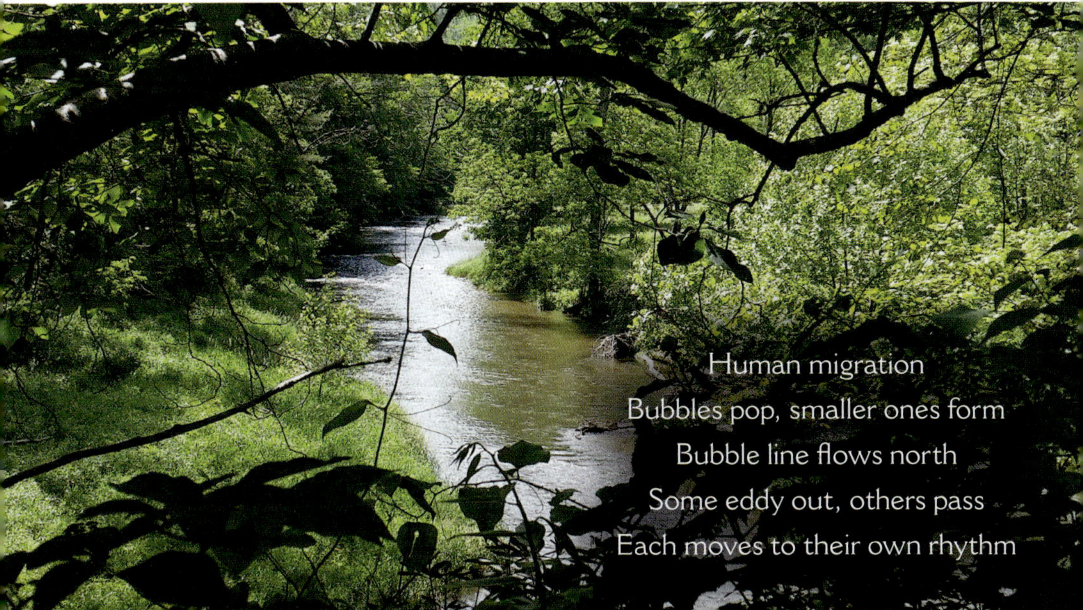

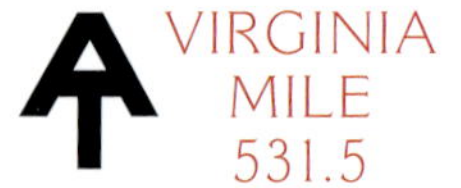

VIRGINIA
MILE
531.5

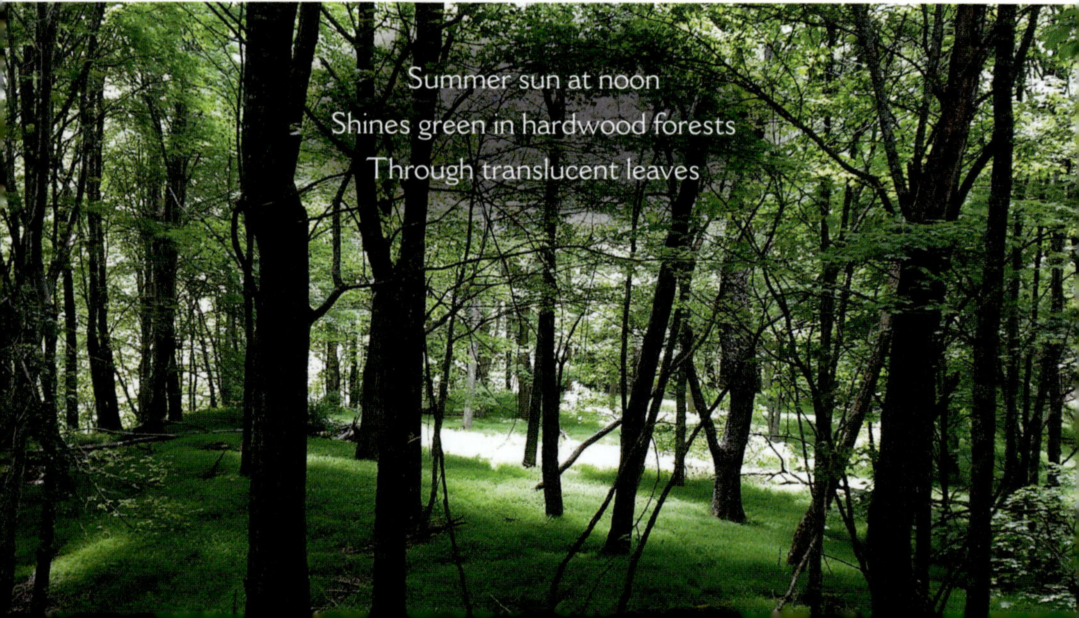

Summer sun at noon
Shines green in hardwood forests
Through translucent leaves

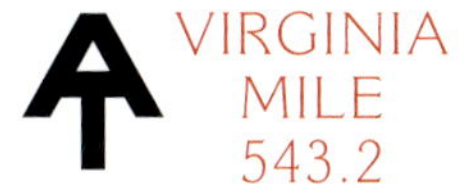

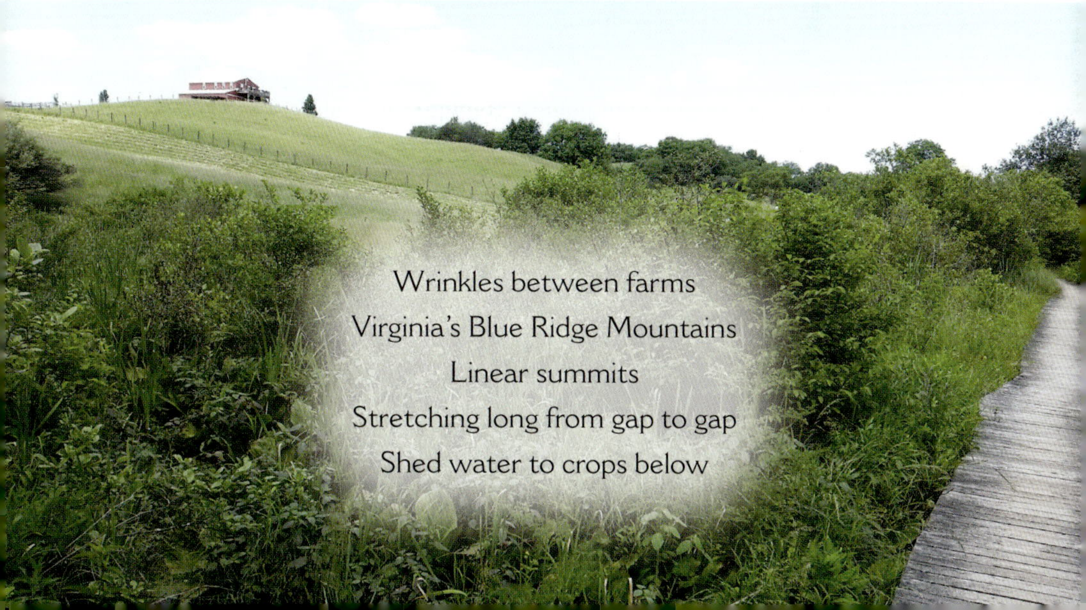

Wrinkles between farms
Virginia's Blue Ridge Mountains
Linear summits
Stretching long from gap to gap
Shed water to crops below

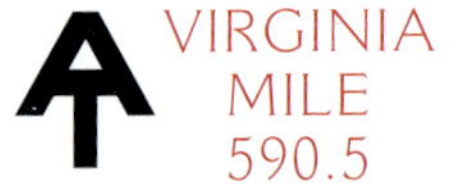

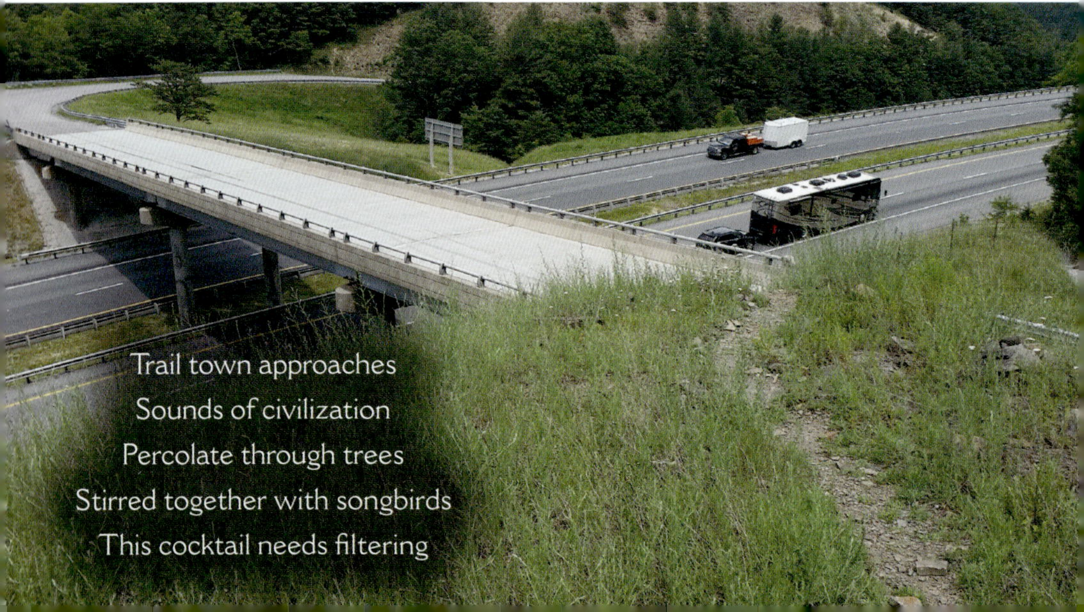

Trail town approaches
Sounds of civilization
Percolate through trees
Stirred together with songbirds
This cocktail needs filtering

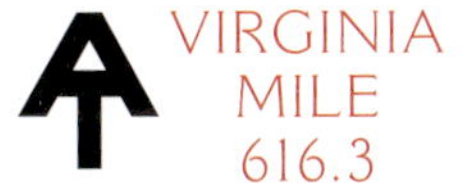

VIRGINIA
MILE
616.3

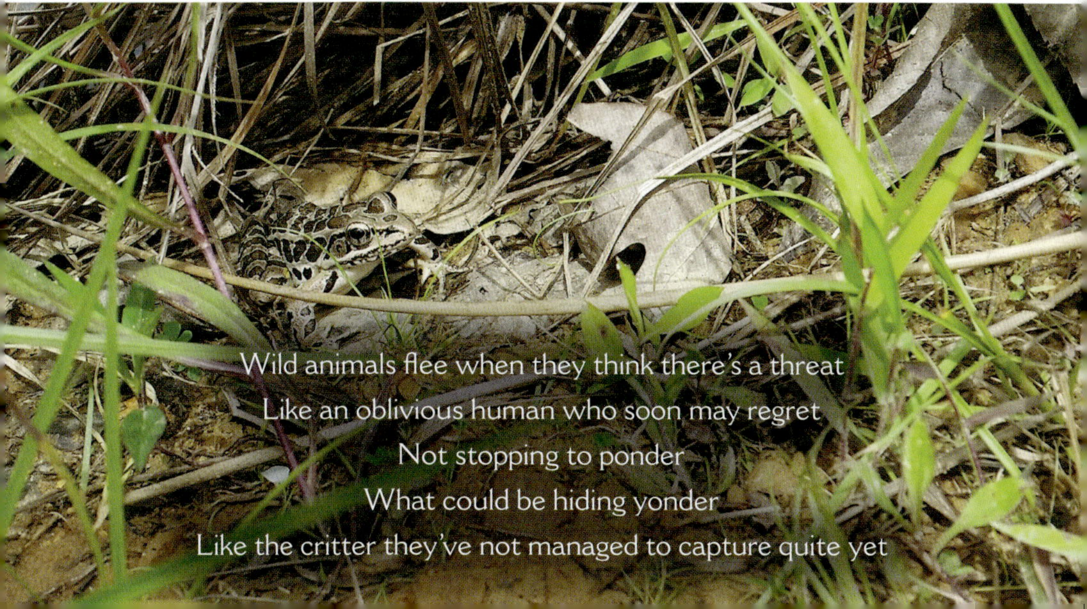

Wild animals flee when they think there's a threat
Like an oblivious human who soon may regret
Not stopping to ponder
What could be hiding yonder
Like the critter they've not managed to capture quite yet

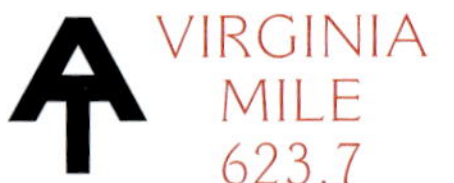

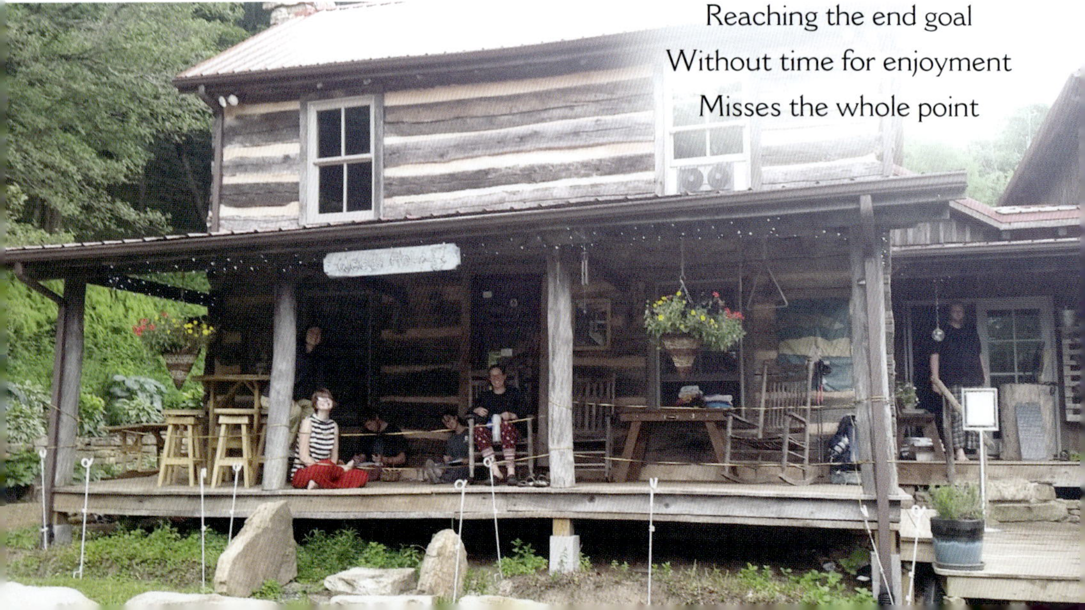

Reaching the end goal
Without time for enjoyment
Misses the whole point

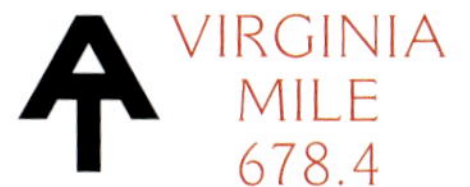

First black raspberries
Hidden in poison ivy
Carefully pick … yum!
Each one tastes slightly different
Nature's variety pack

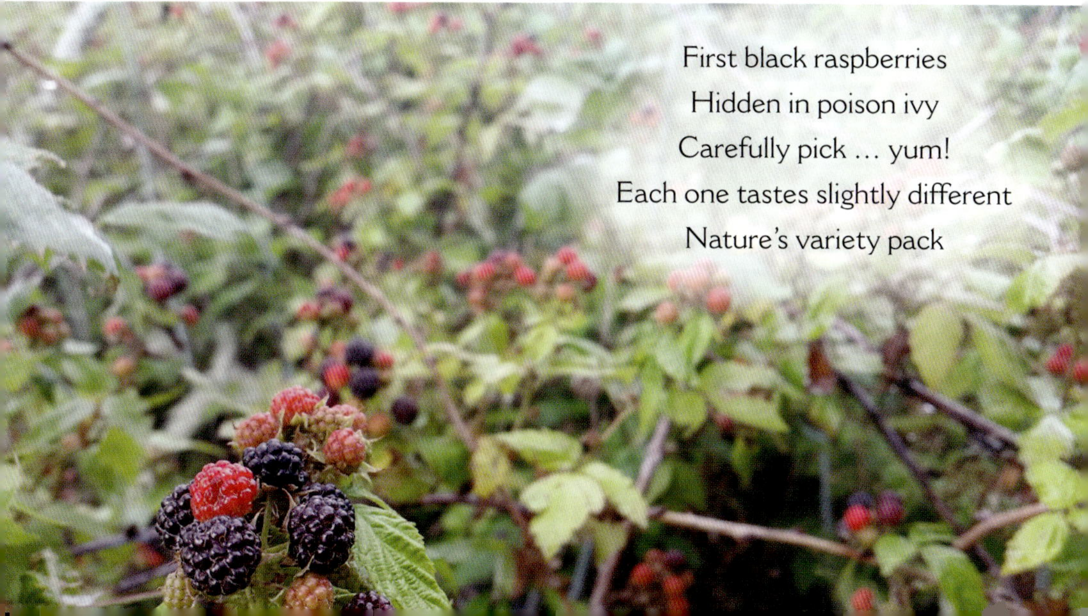

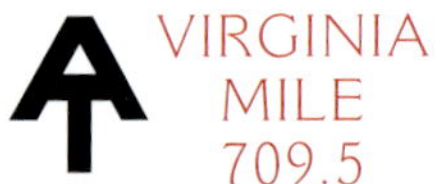

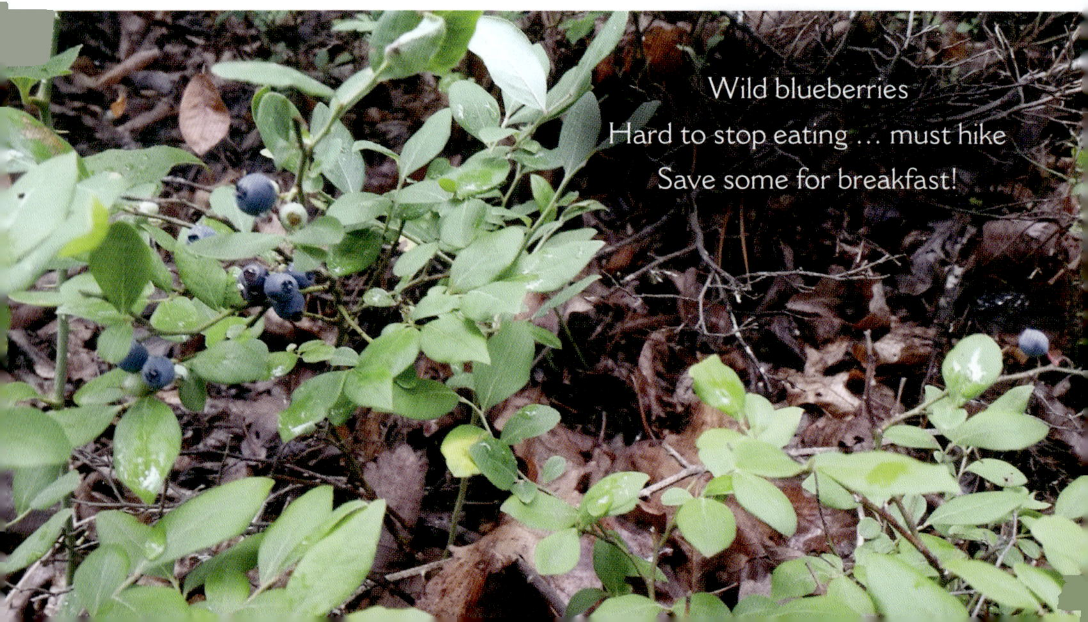

Wild blueberries
Hard to stop eating ... must hike
Save some for breakfast!

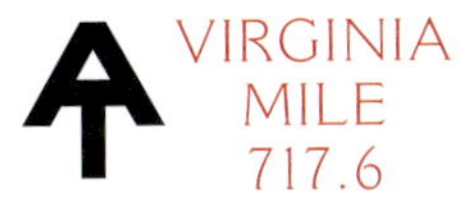

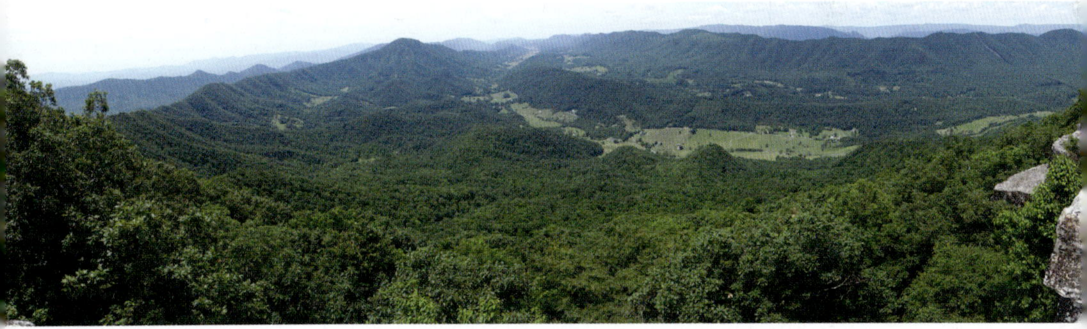

Treetops at my feet
Farmland and ridgelines below
Hawk flies straight at me
Where I've been and yet to go
Meander on Tinker Cliffs

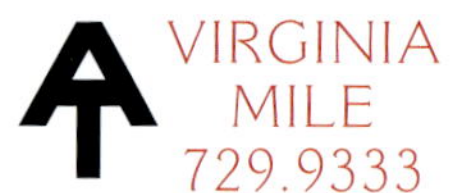

VIRGINIA
MILE
729.9333

I understand why they're called Virginia Blues
Rocky, tough, and slow days with hard-to-earn views
I've come a long way, but there's so far to go
Heading toward Maine, it's a race against snow
Trail is taking its toll
On mind, body, and soul
Balancing time, money, miles, and snooze

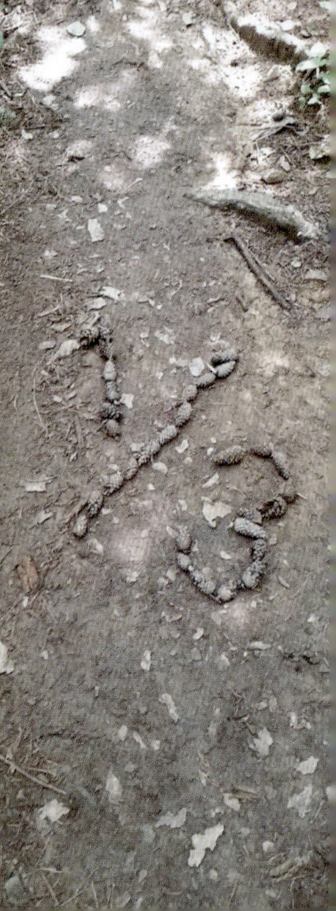

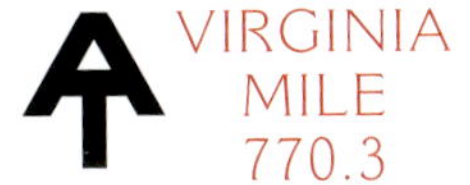

VIRGINIA MILE 770.3

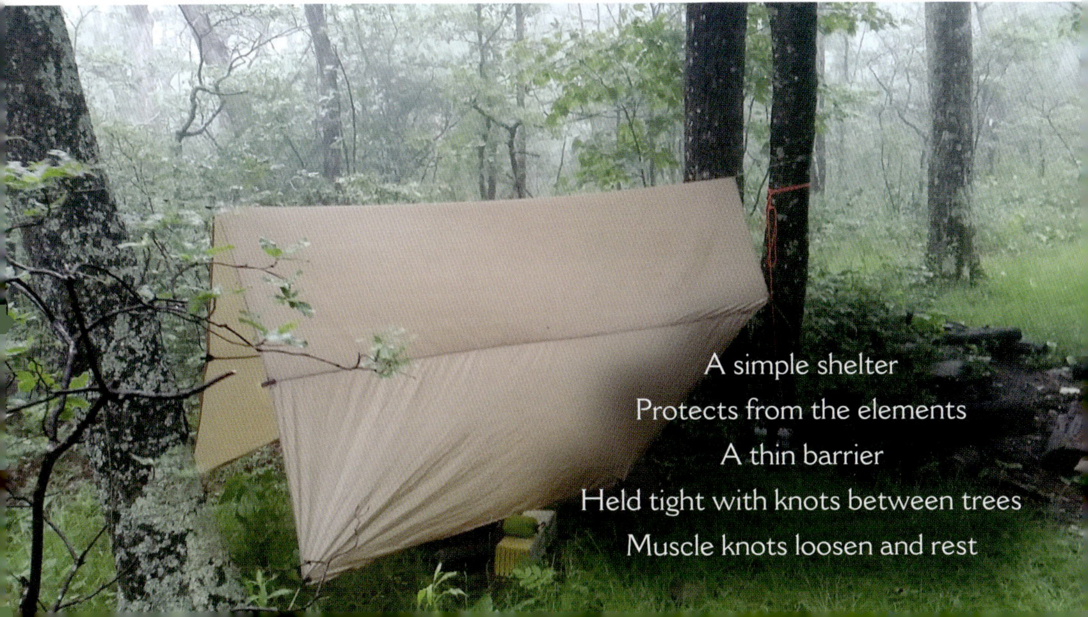

A simple shelter
Protects from the elements
A thin barrier
Held tight with knots between trees
Muscle knots loosen and rest

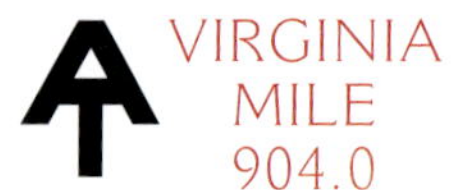

VIRGINIA
MILE
904.0

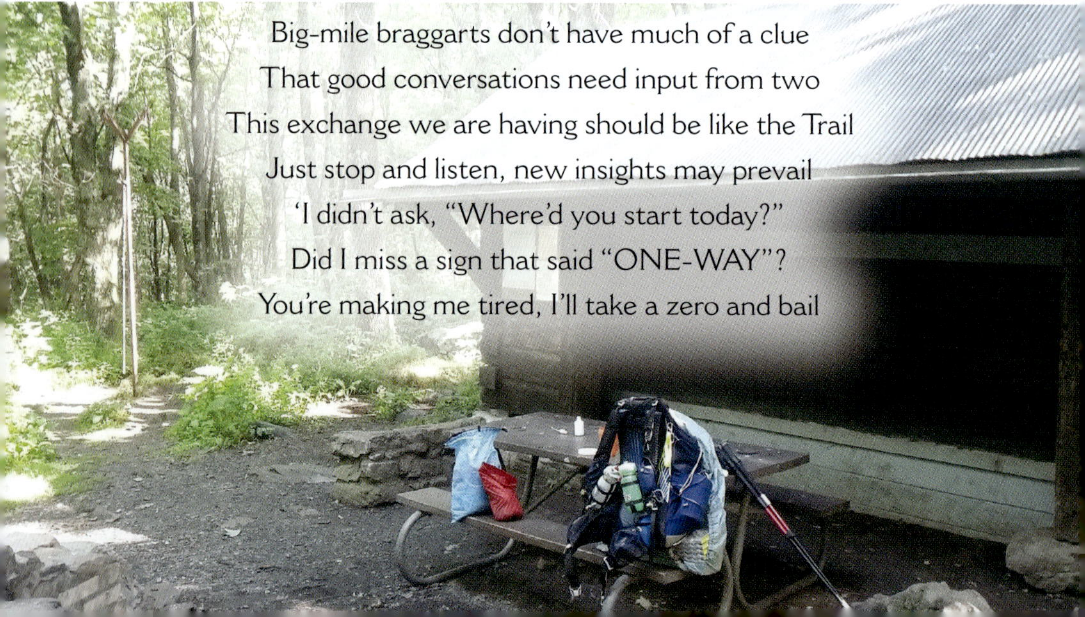

Big-mile braggarts don't have much of a clue
That good conversations need input from two
This exchange we are having should be like the Trail
Just stop and listen, new insights may prevail
'I didn't ask, "Where'd you start today?"
Did I miss a sign that said "ONE-WAY"?
You're making me tired, I'll take a zero and bail

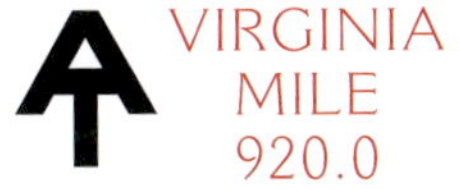

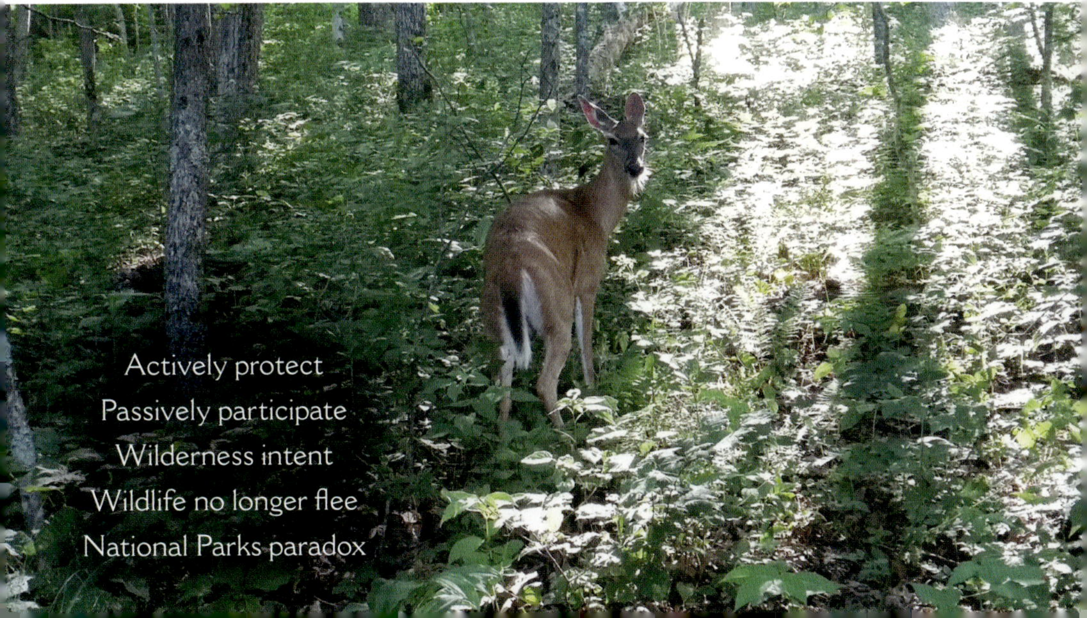

Actively protect
Passively participate
Wilderness intent
Wildlife no longer flee
National Parks paradox

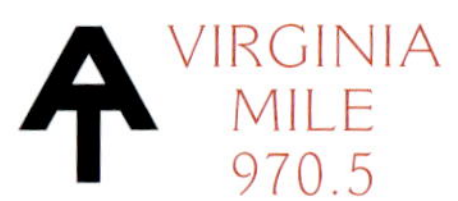

Wineberries galore!
Emerge from fuzzy cocoons
Sweaty fingers pluck

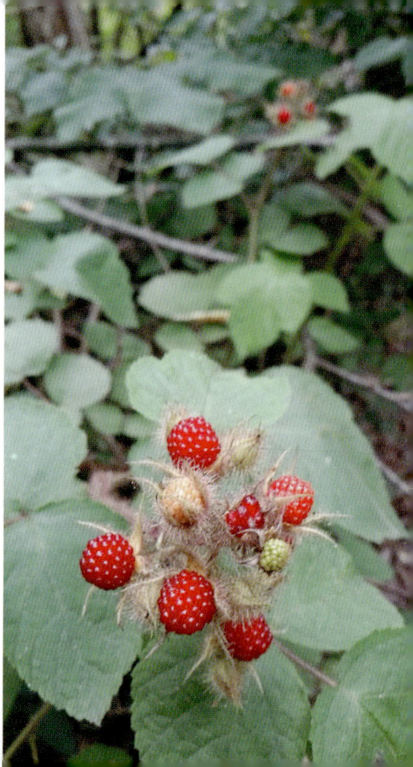

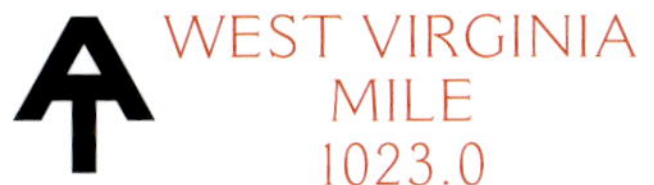

WEST VIRGINIA
MILE
1023.0

Milestone observed
Harpers Ferry zero day
This glass is half-full

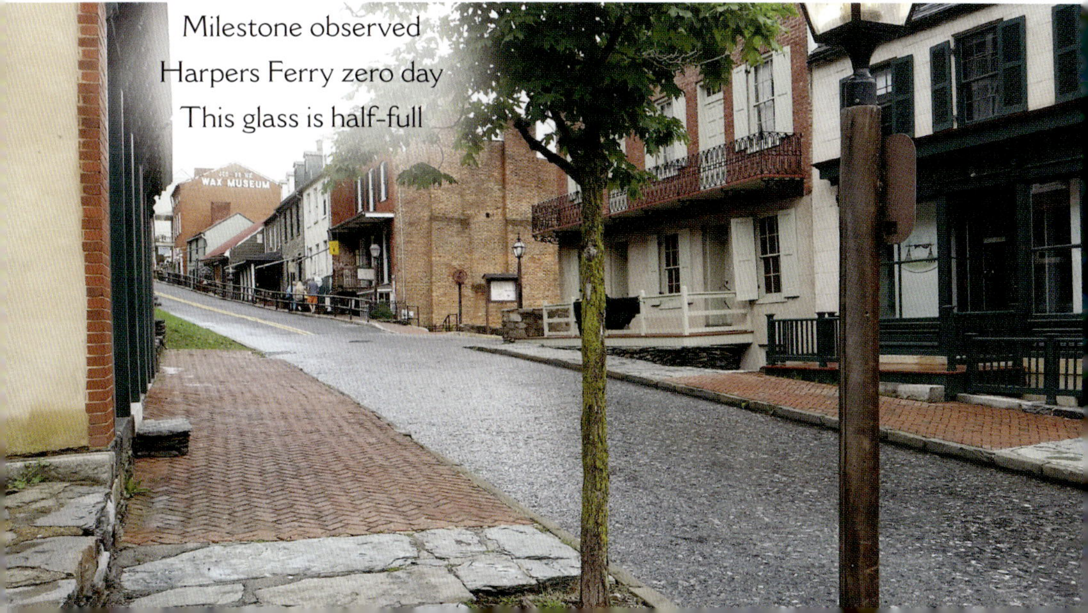

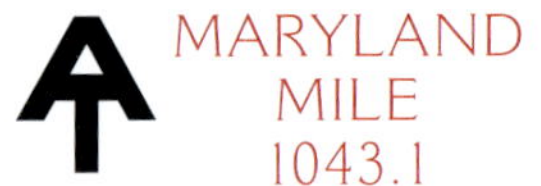

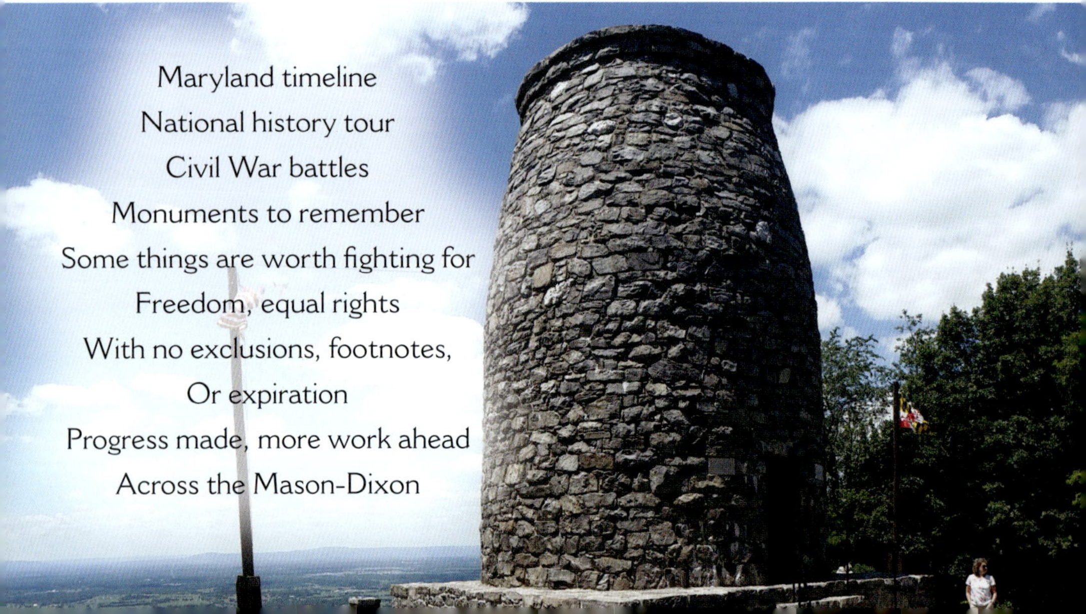

Maryland timeline
National history tour
Civil War battles
Monuments to remember
Some things are worth fighting for
Freedom, equal rights
With no exclusions, footnotes,
Or expiration
Progress made, more work ahead
Across the Mason-Dixon

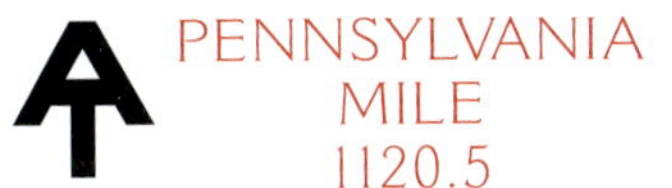

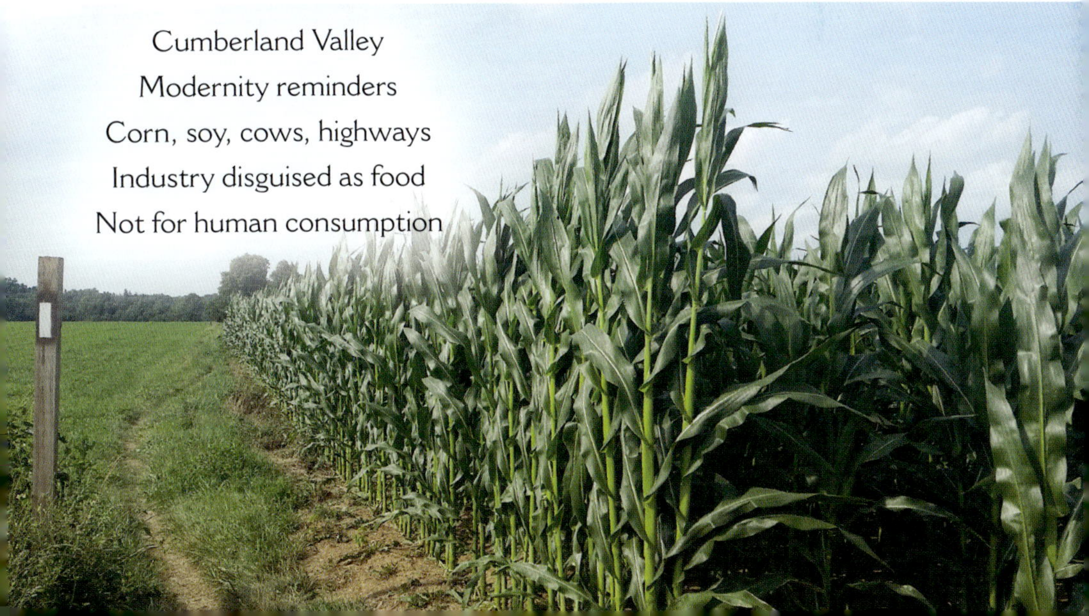

Cumberland Valley
Modernity reminders
Corn, soy, cows, highways
Industry disguised as food
Not for human consumption

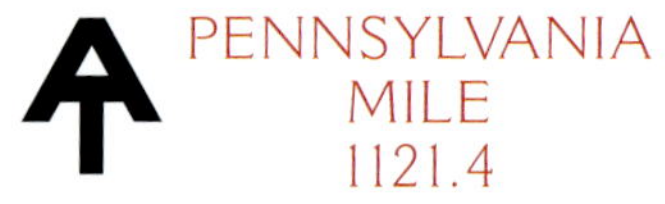

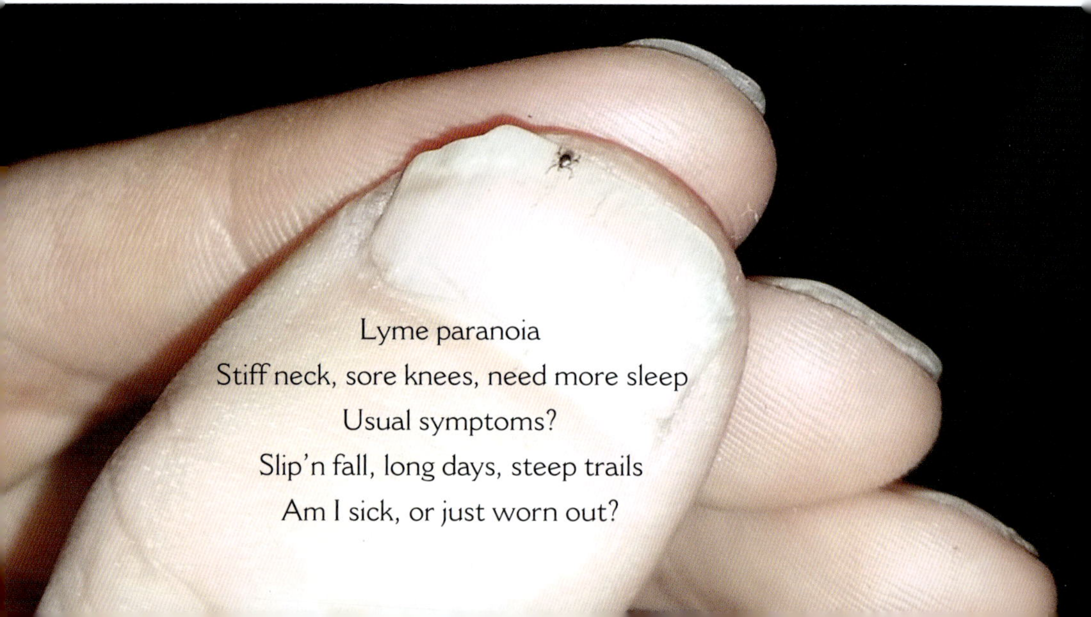

Lyme paranoia
Stiff neck, sore knees, need more sleep
Usual symptoms?
Slip'n fall, long days, steep trails
Am I sick, or just worn out?

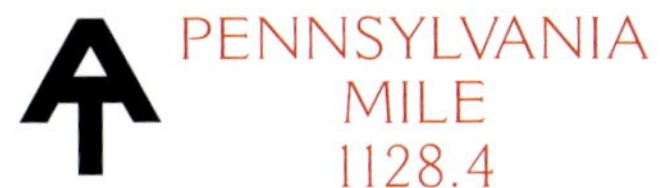

PENNSYLVANIA
MILE
1128.4

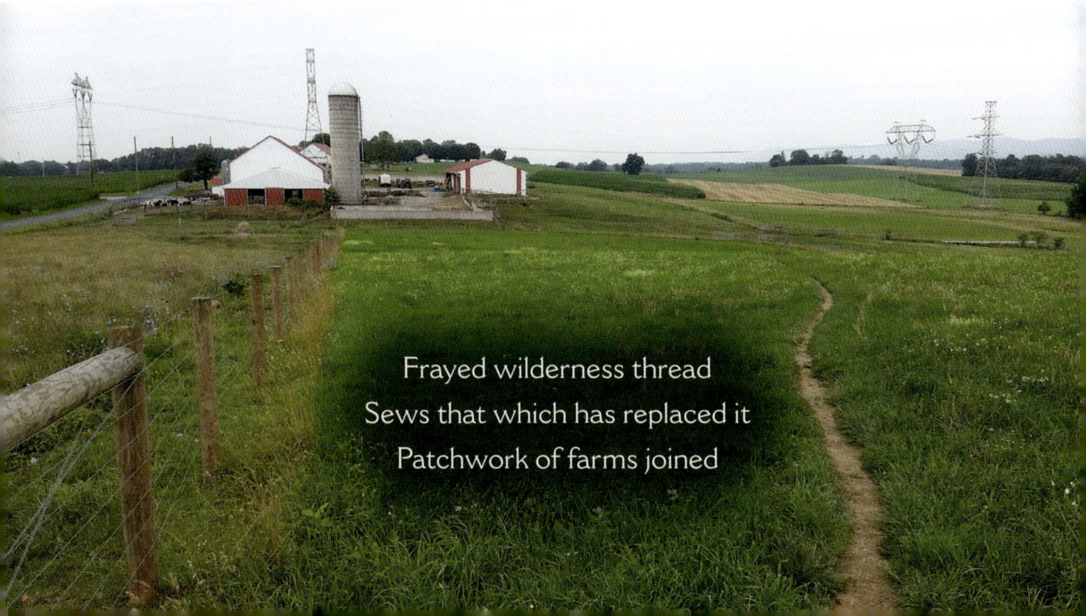

Frayed wilderness thread
Sews that which has replaced it
Patchwork of farms joined

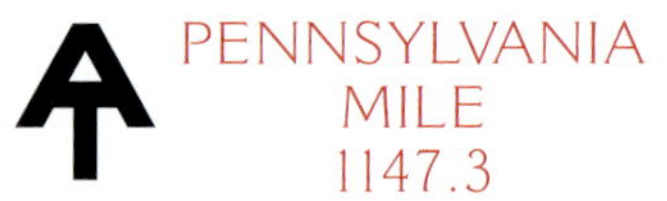

PENNSYLVANIA
MILE
1147.3

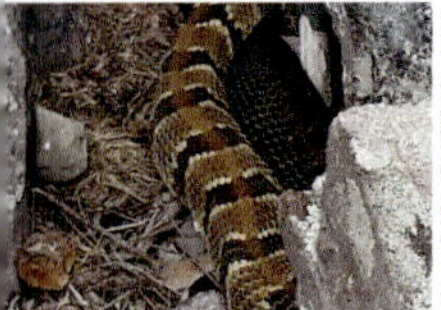
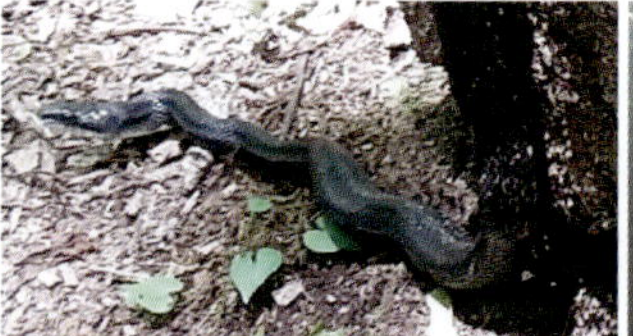
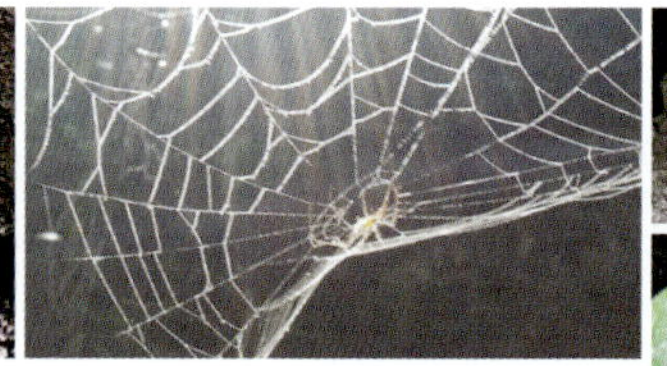
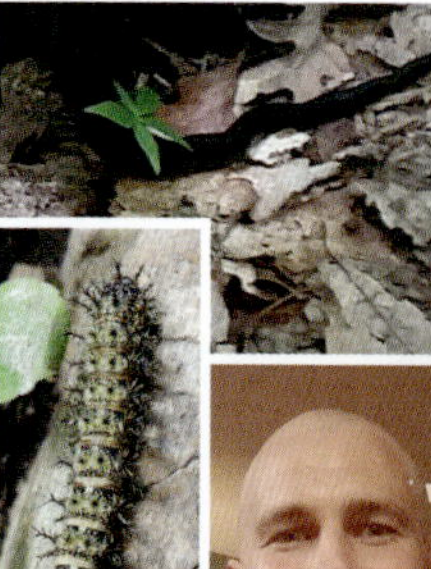
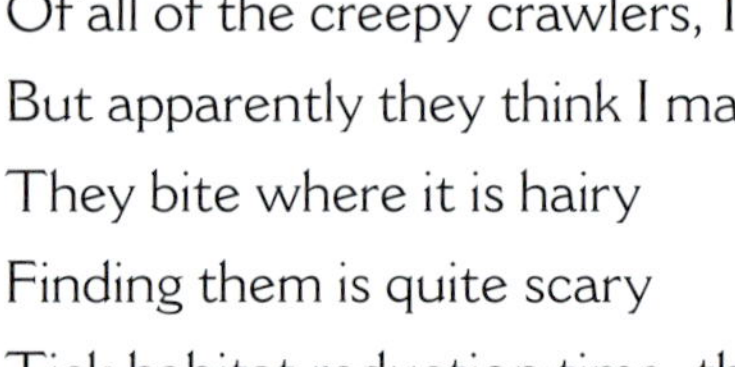

Of all of the creepy crawlers, I despise ticks the most
But apparently they think I make a pretty good host
They bite where it is hairy
Finding them is quite scary
Tick habitat reduction time, this 'fro and beard of mine are toast!

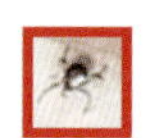
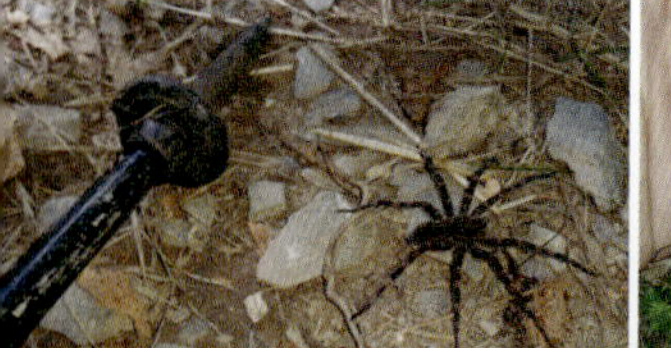
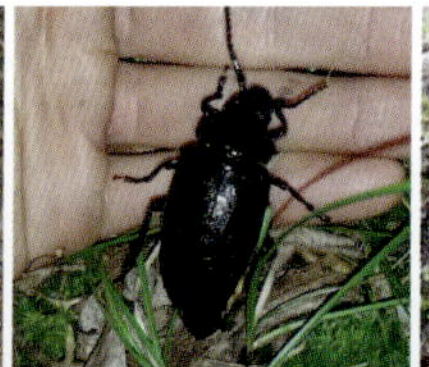
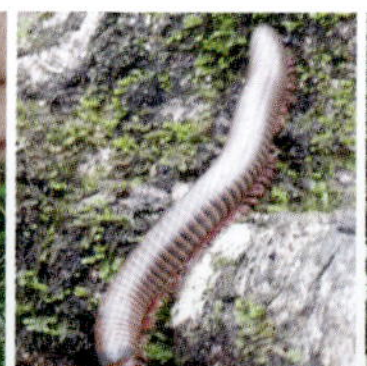
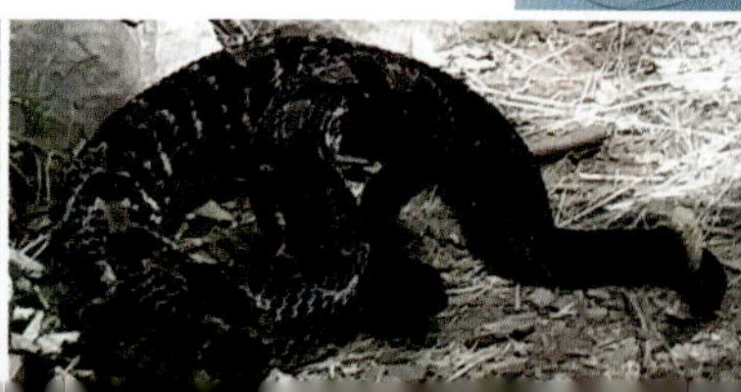

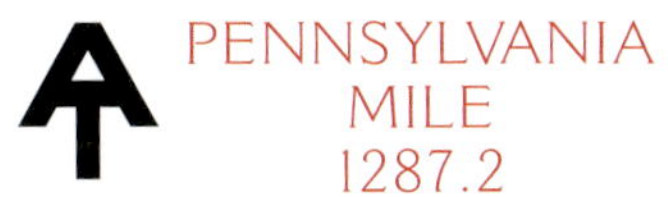

PENNSYLVANIA
MILE
1287.2

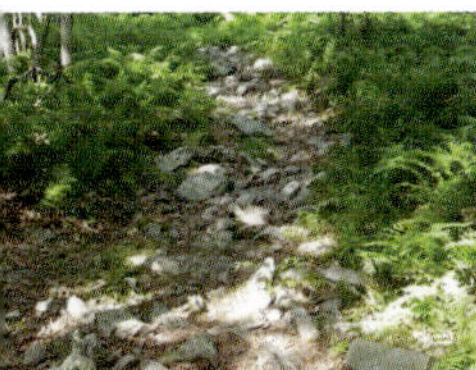
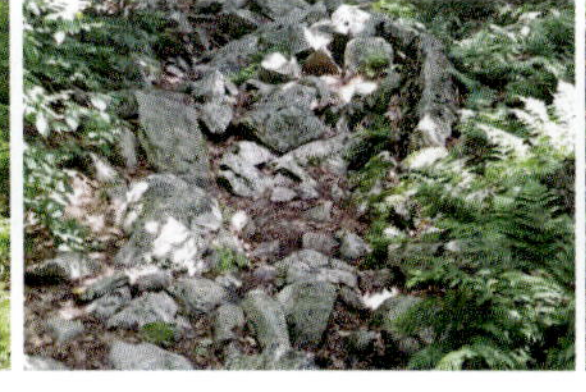
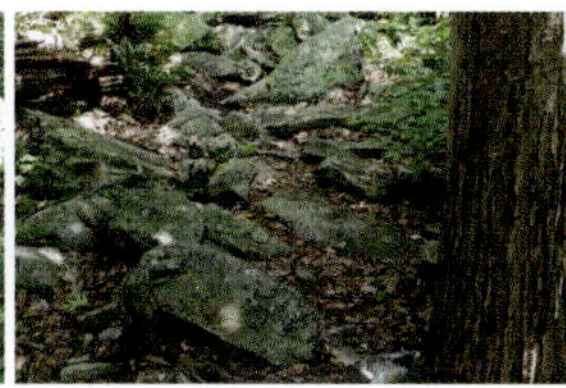
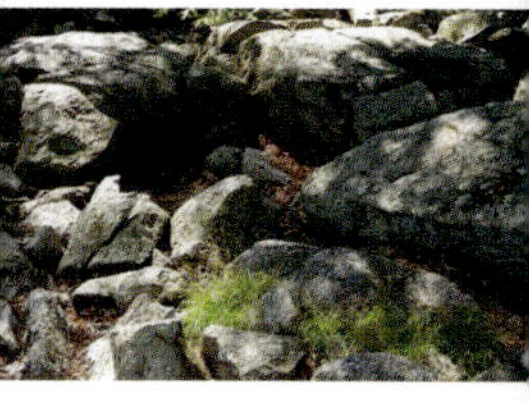

If Pennsylvania sang opera, it would be monotoned. If Pennsylvania were hard candy, its flavor would be all-purpose white flour. If Pennsylvania were a children's book, there would be no illustrations. If Pennsylvania went on a date, it would wear bear-spray perfume. If Pennsylvania were your bed sheets, they'd be hot, wet, and sticky latex. If Pennsylvania had a saving grace, it's the amazing trail magic!

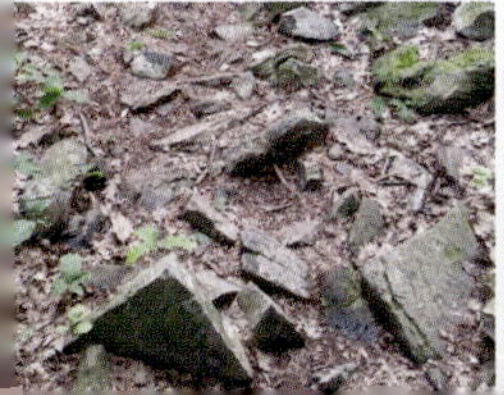
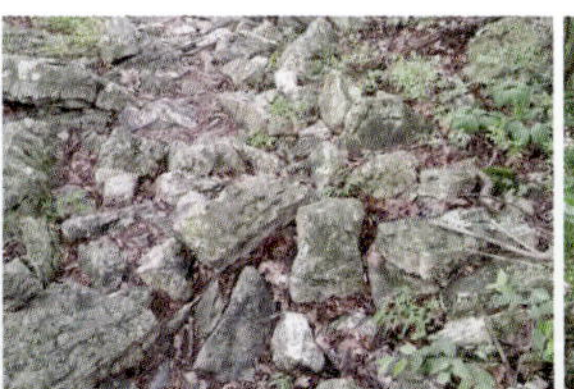
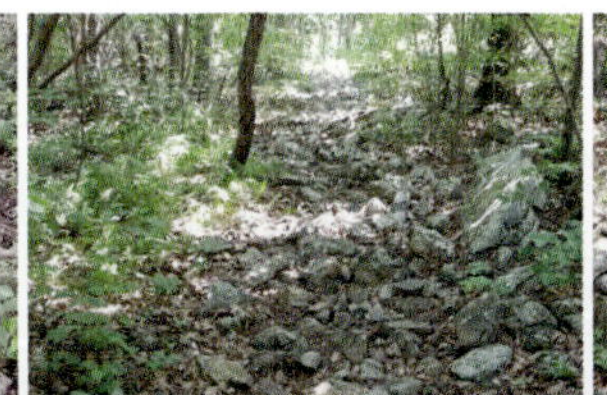
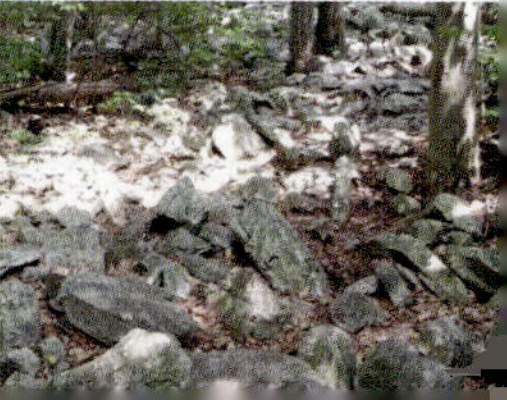

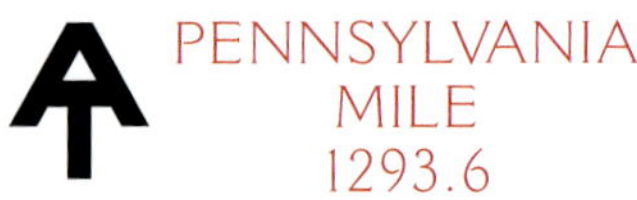

PENNSYLVANIA MILE 1293.6

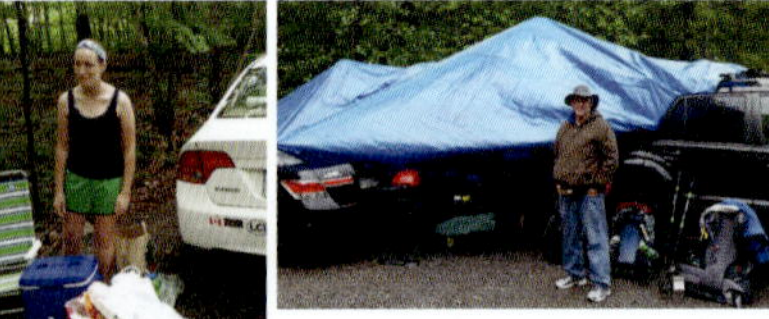

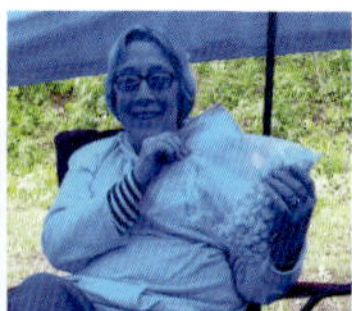

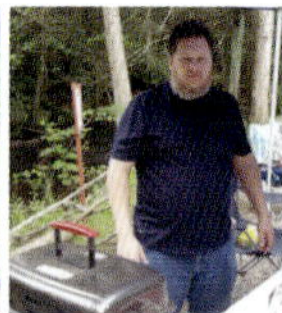

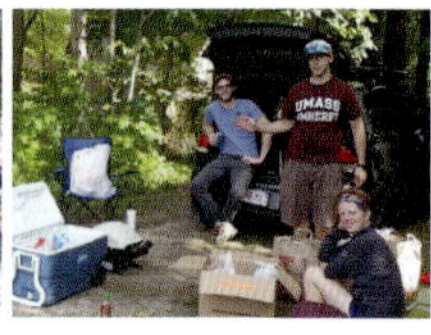

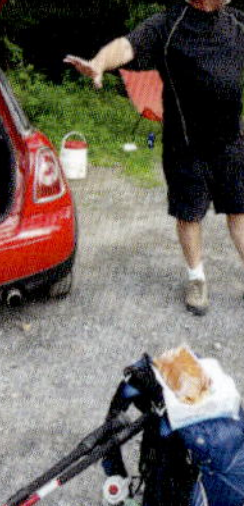

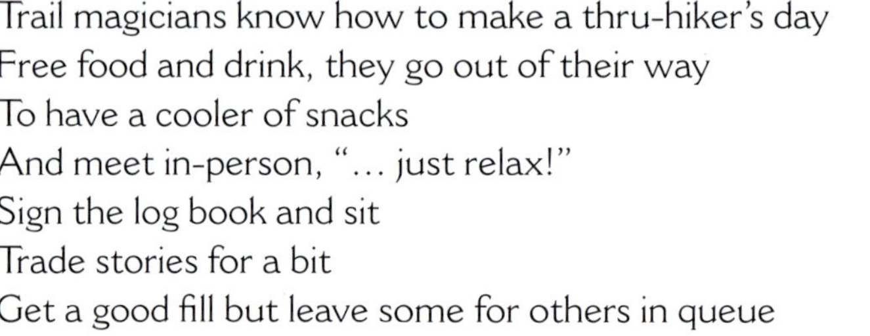

Trail magicians know how to make a thru-hiker's day
Free food and drink, they go out of their way
To have a cooler of snacks
And meet in-person, "… just relax!"
Sign the log book and sit
Trade stories for a bit
Get a good fill but leave some for others in queue
Give a fist-bump farewell and be sure to say, "Thank you!"

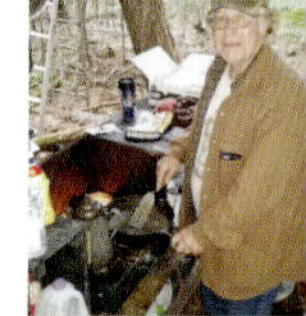

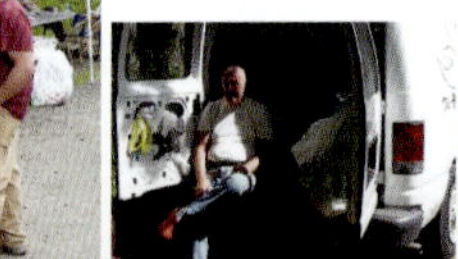

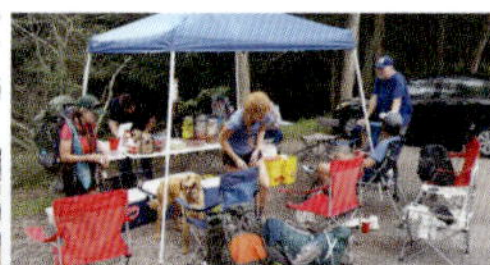

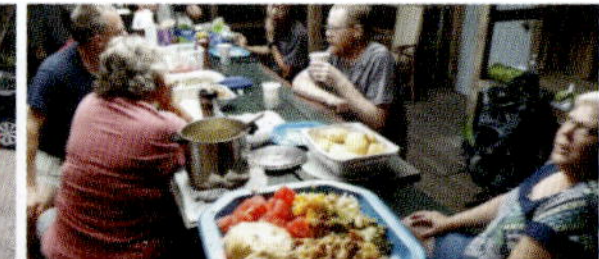

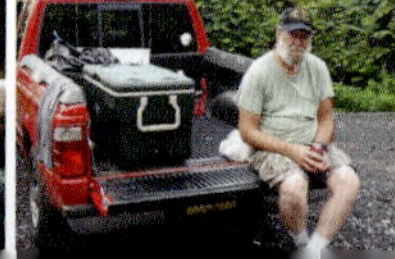

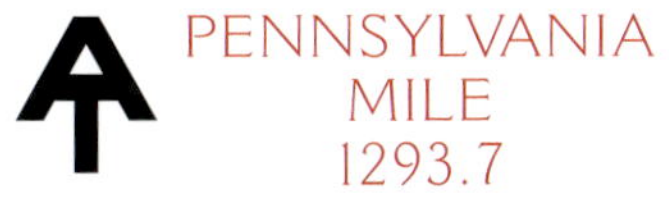

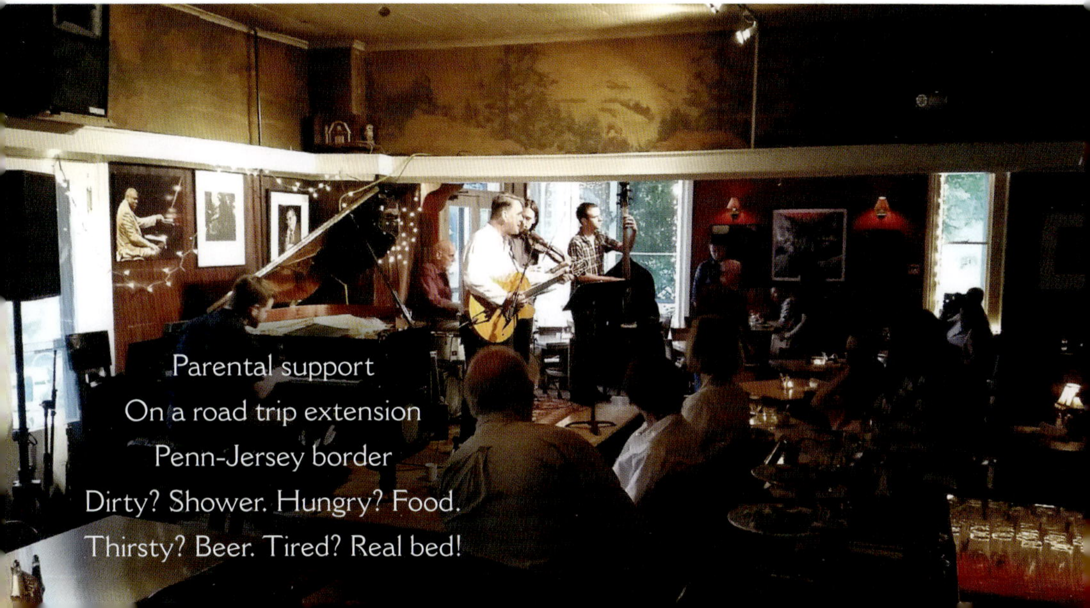

Parental support

On a road trip extension

Penn-Jersey border

Dirty? Shower. Hungry? Food.

Thirsty? Beer. Tired? Real bed!

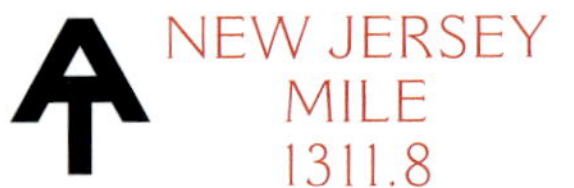

NEW JERSEY MILE 1311.8

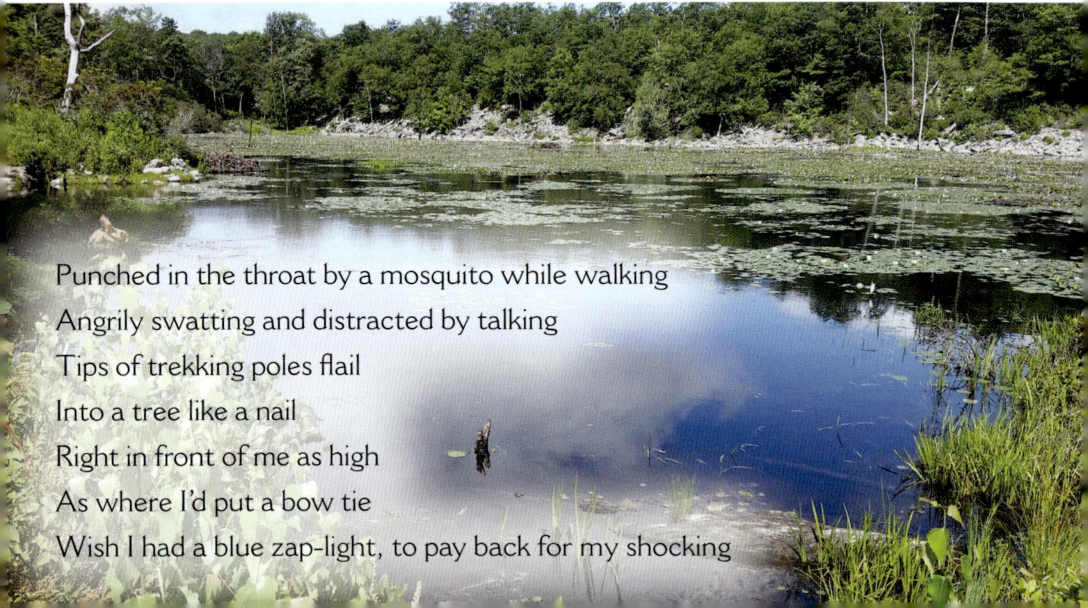

Punched in the throat by a mosquito while walking
Angrily swatting and distracted by talking
Tips of trekking poles flail
Into a tree like a nail
Right in front of me as high
As where I'd put a bow tie
Wish I had a blue zap-light, to pay back for my shocking

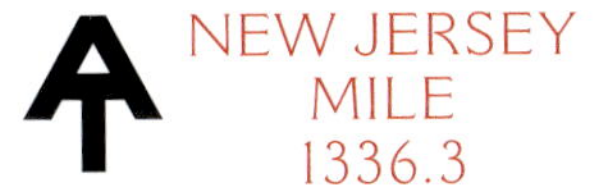

NEW JERSEY MILE 1336.3

Cold, torrential rain
Bad timing for morning poop
Dig hole – tons of roots
Wiping a magic marker?
TP dissolving in hands
4-day supply … gone
Rain pants don't work when they're down
When everything's soaked
Dry ankles go unnoticed
Cold, shaved head misses afro

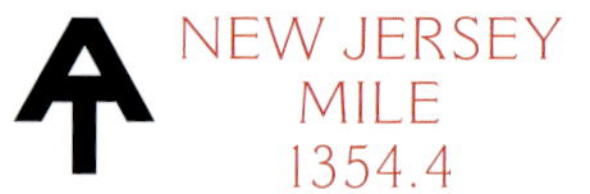

NEW JERSEY
MILE
1354.4

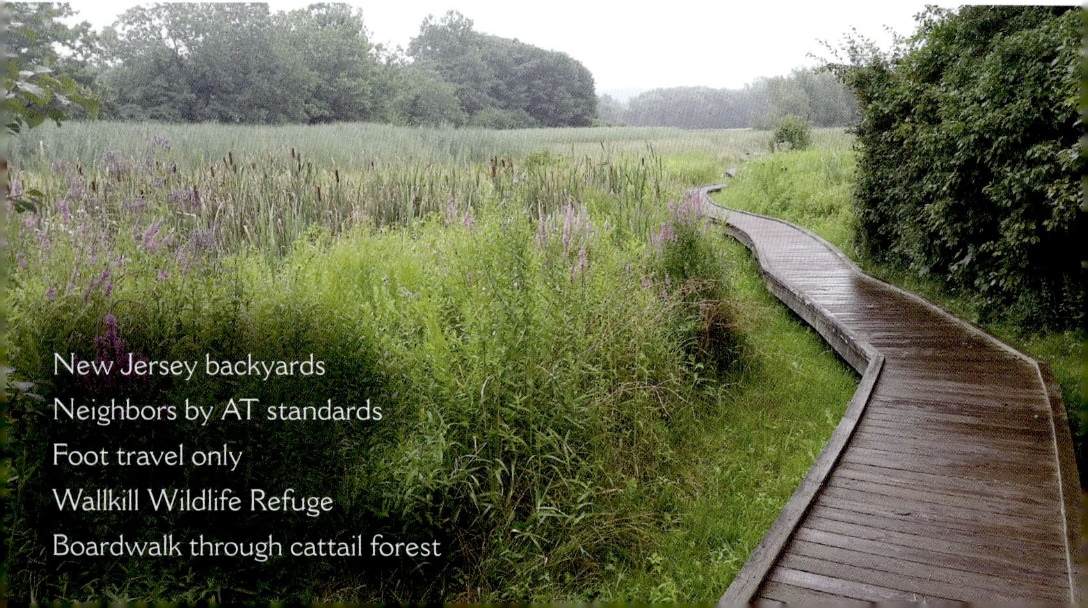

New Jersey backyards

Neighbors by AT standards

Foot travel only

Wallkill Wildlife Refuge

Boardwalk through cattail forest

NEW YORK
MILE
1386.2

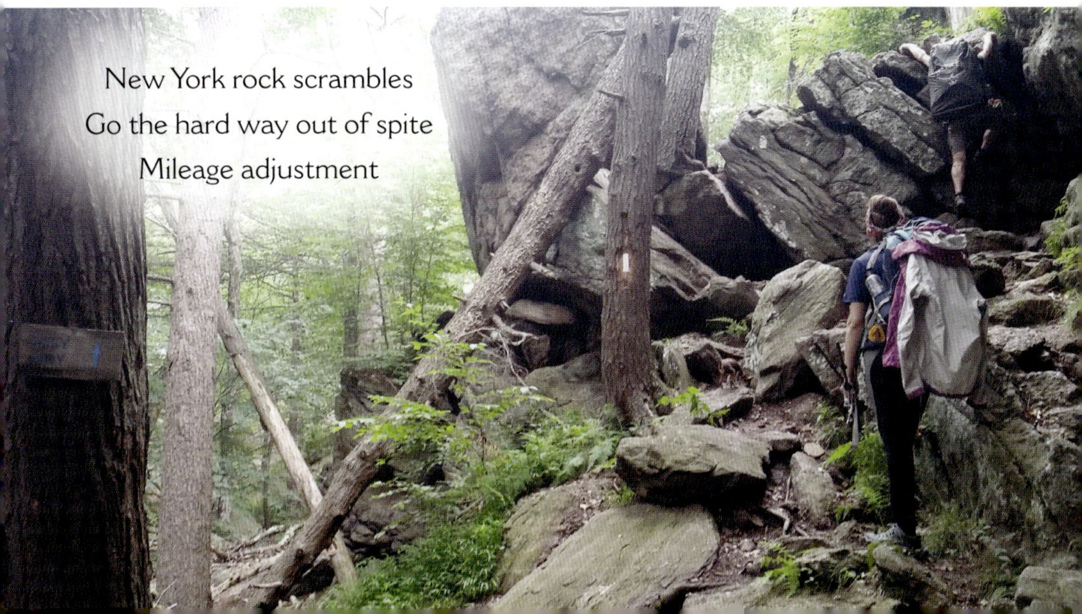

New York rock scrambles
Go the hard way out of spite
Mileage adjustment

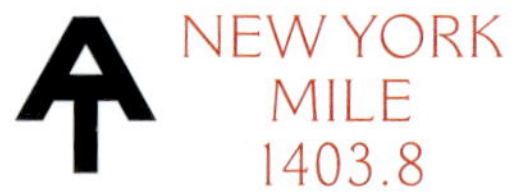

NEW YORK
MILE
1403.8

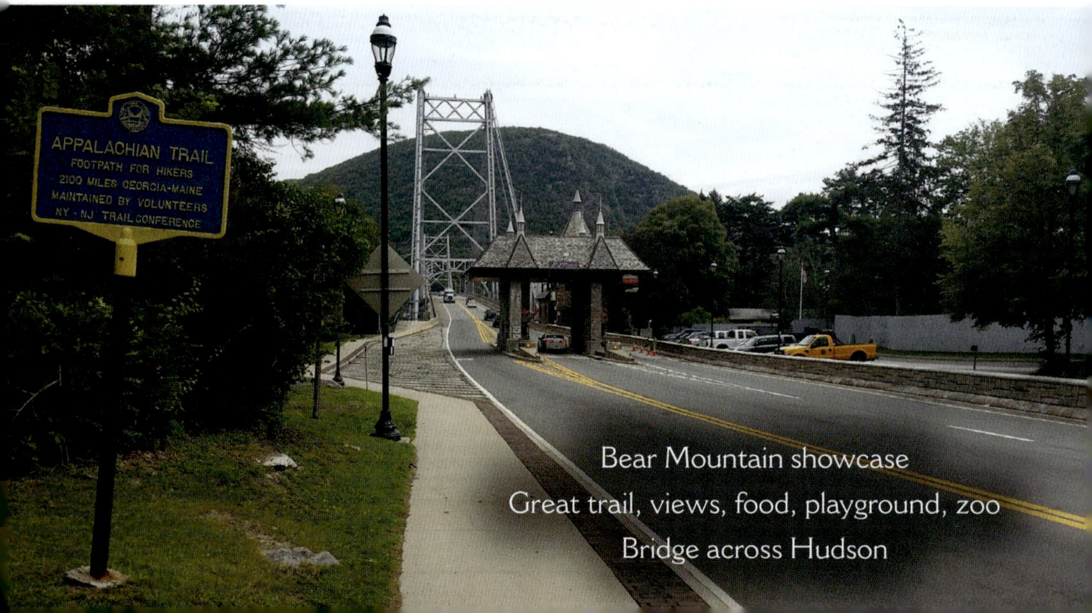

Bear Mountain showcase

Great trail, views, food, playground, zoo

Bridge across Hudson

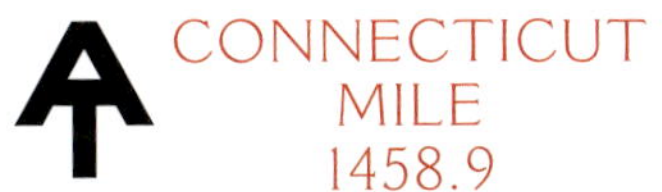

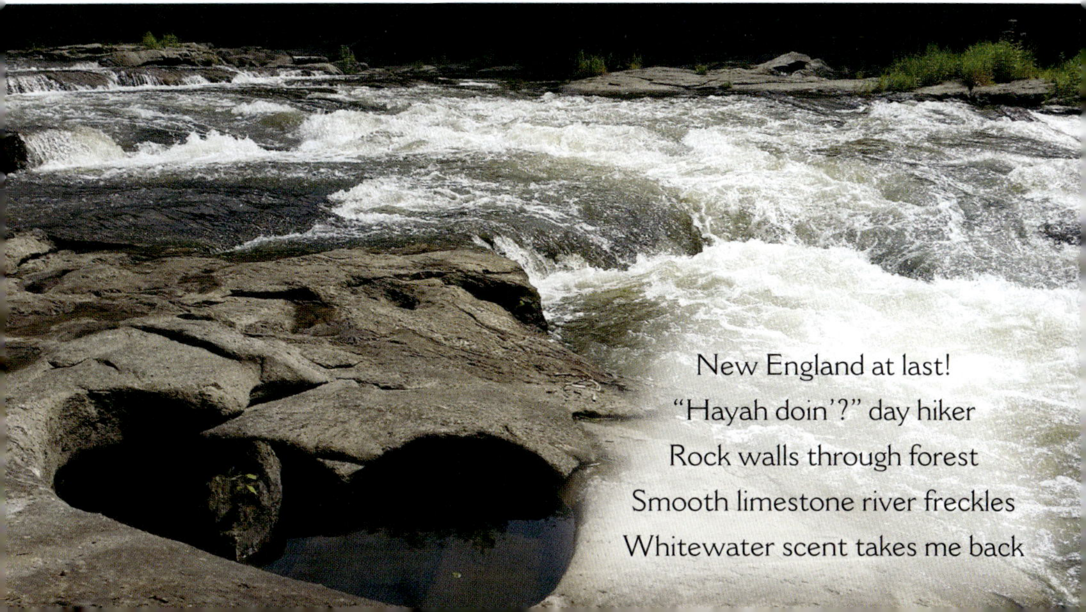

New England at last!
"Hayah doin'?" day hiker
Rock walls through forest
Smooth limestone river freckles
Whitewater scent takes me back

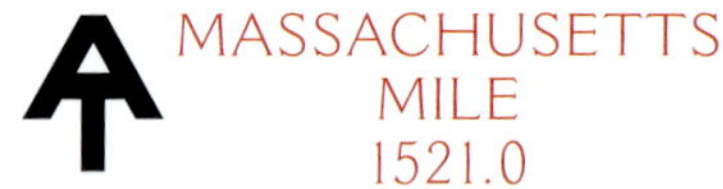

MASSACHUSETTS
MILE
1521.0

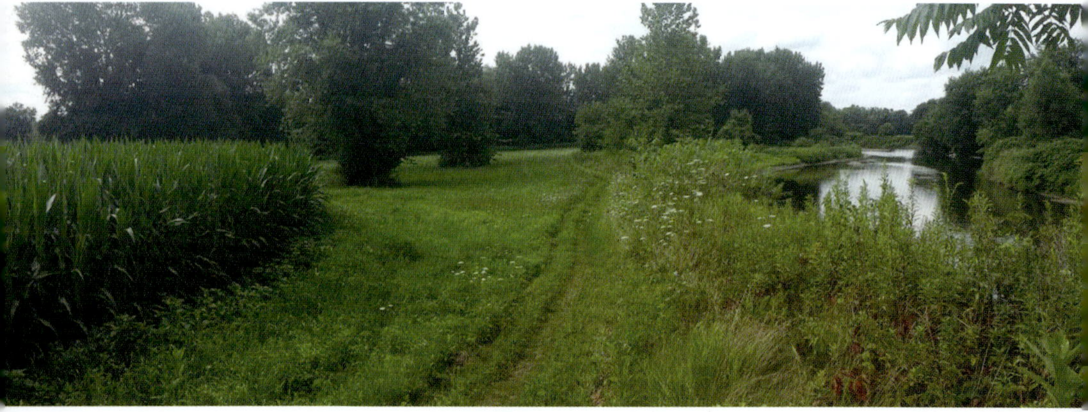

Following river
Wandering Housatonic
Flat water to falls

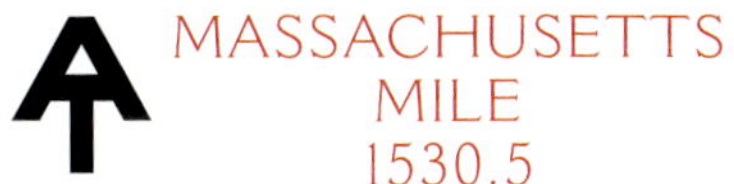

MASSACHUSETTS MILE 1530.5

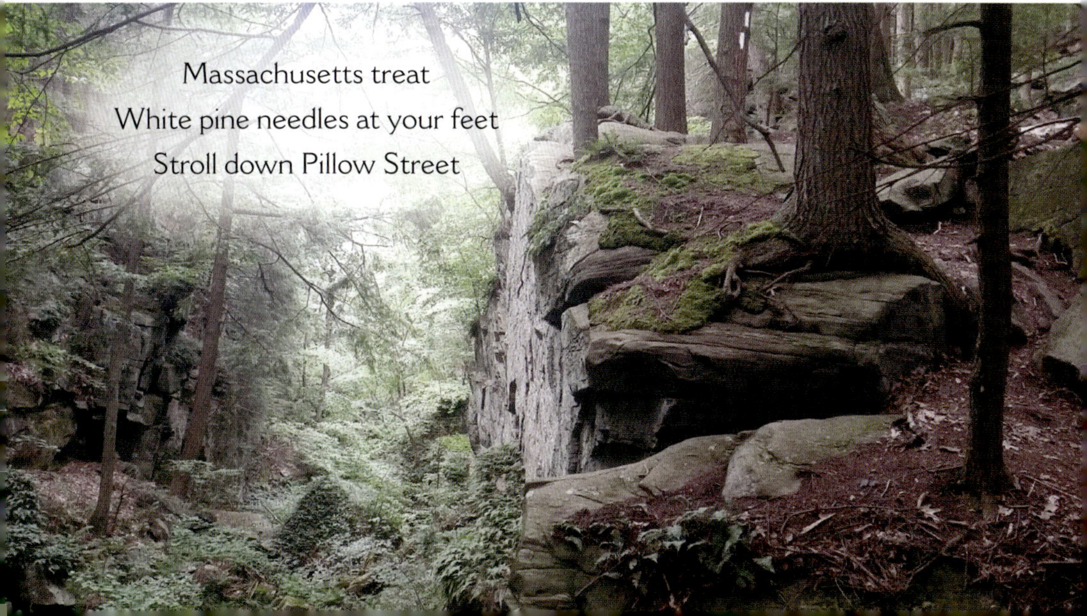

Massachusetts treat
White pine needles at your feet
Stroll down Pillow Street

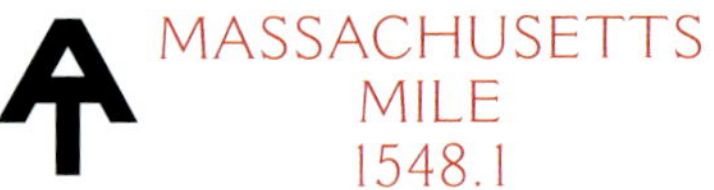

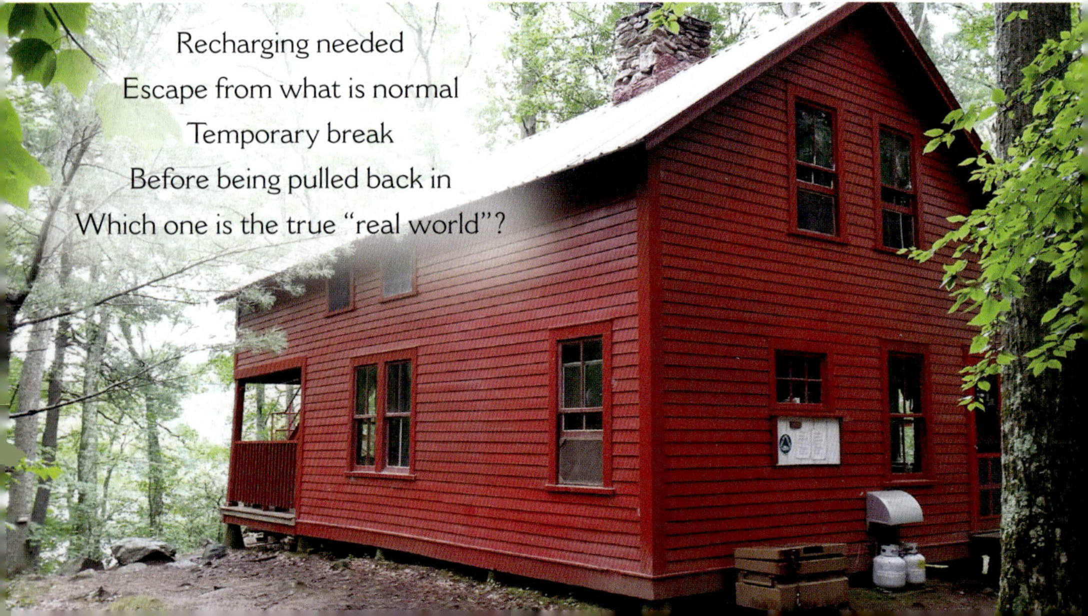

Recharging needed
Escape from what is normal
Temporary break
Before being pulled back in
Which one is the true "real world"?

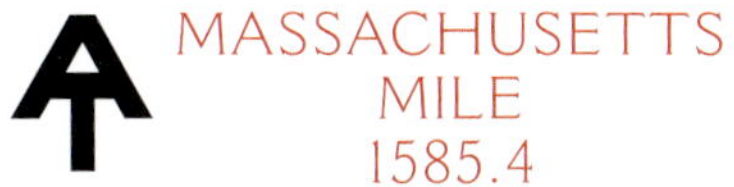

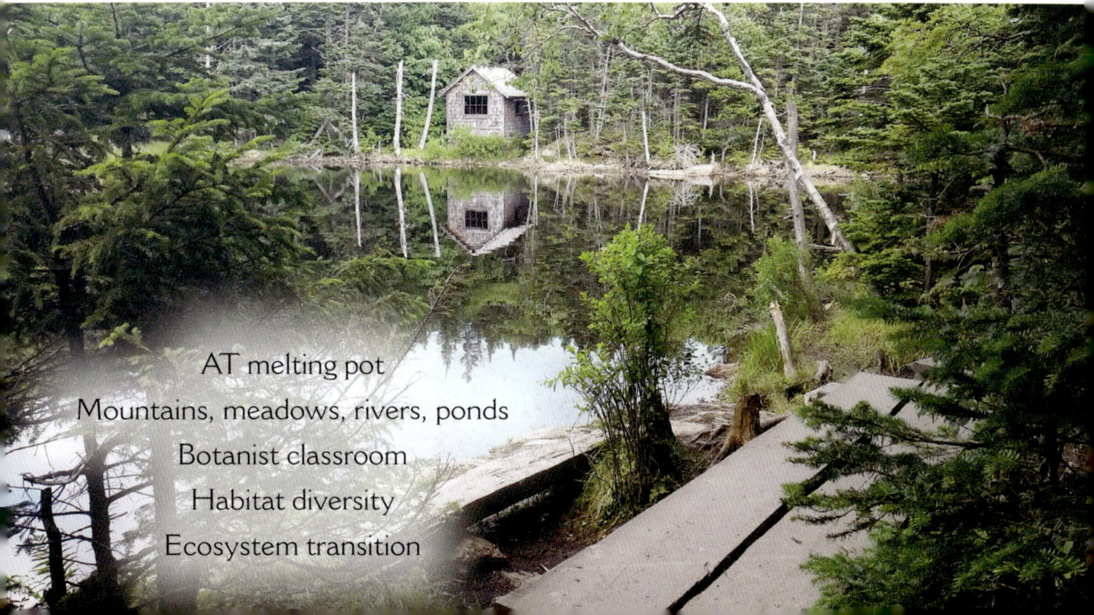

AT melting pot

Mountains, meadows, rivers, ponds

Botanist classroom

Habitat diversity

Ecosystem transition

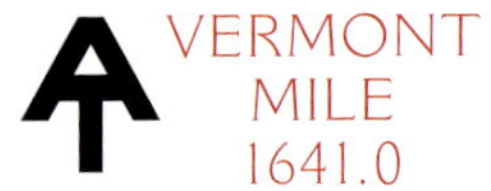

VERMONT
MILE
1641.0

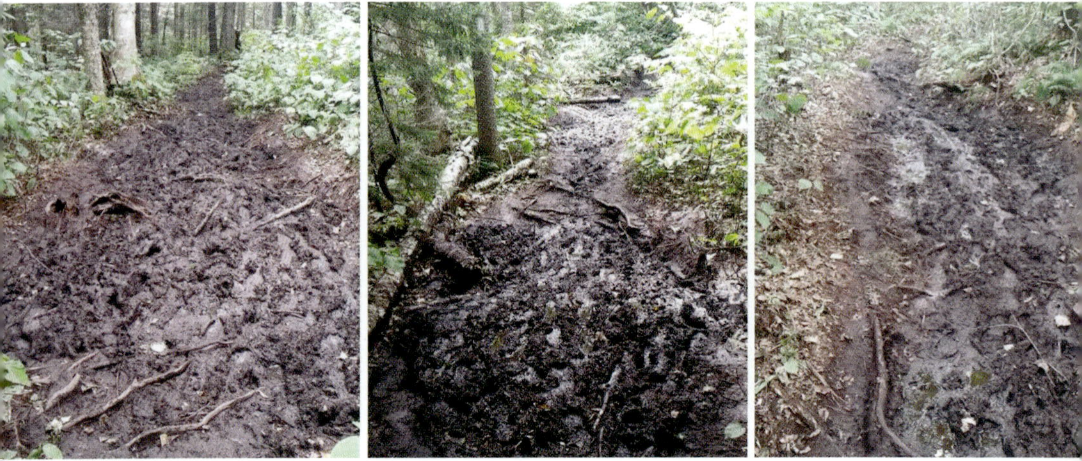

Vermont mud crossings. Boot-print pools in cookie dough. Greasy footsteps slip.
Epic spills make a splatter. Covered in brownie batter.

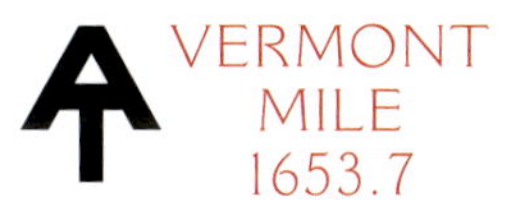

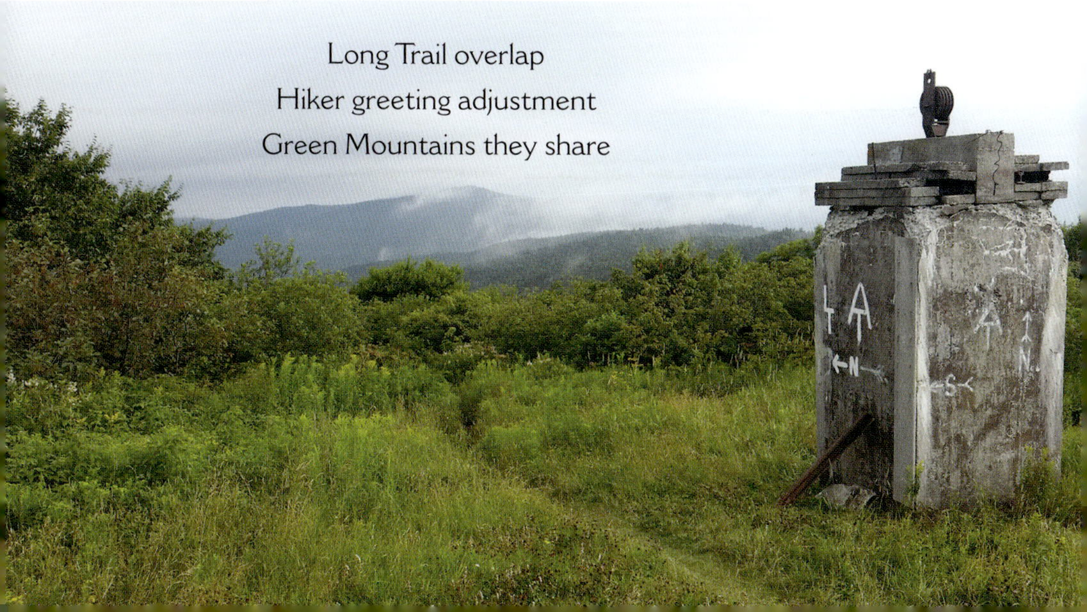

Long Trail overlap
Hiker greeting adjustment
Green Mountains they share

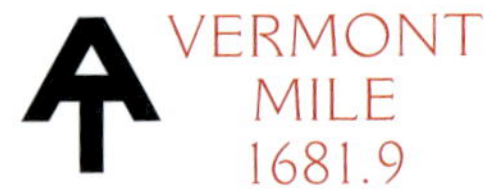

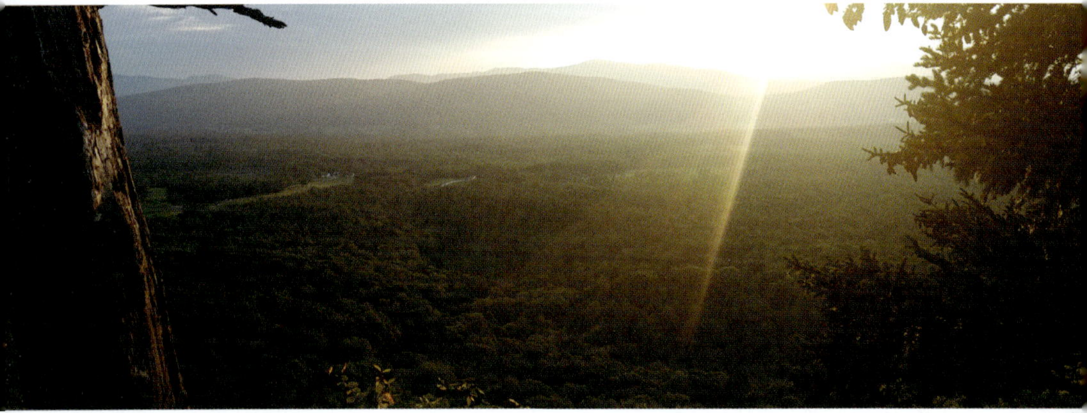

Peek-a-boo through trees
With a late afternoon sun
Long shadow glimpses

VERMONT
MILE
1728.1

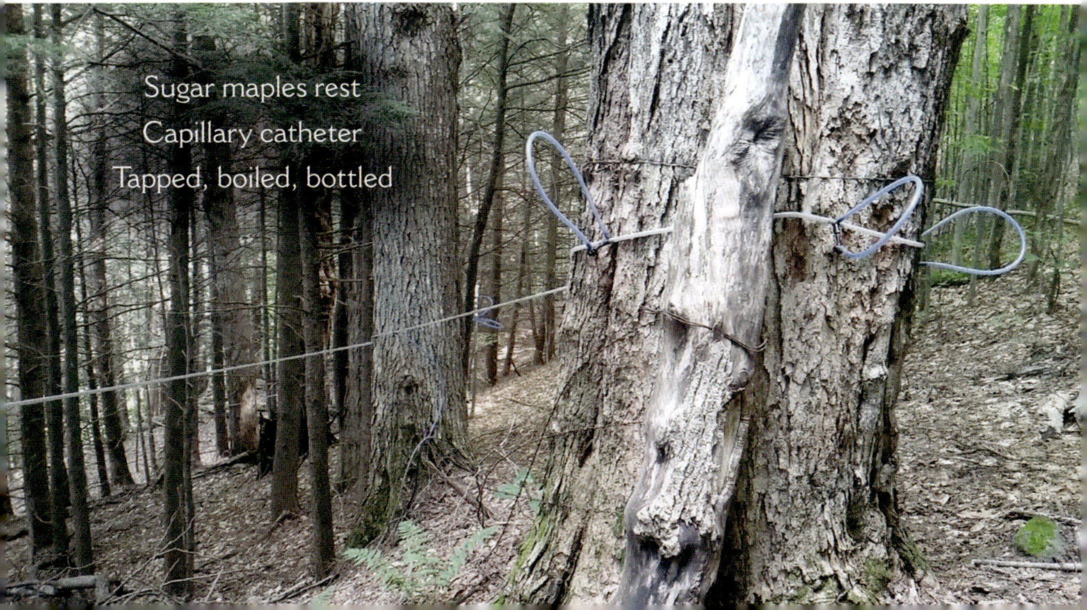

Sugar maples rest
Capillary catheter
Tapped, boiled, bottled

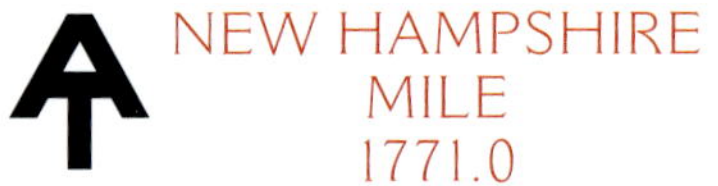

NEW HAMPSHIRE
MILE
1771.0

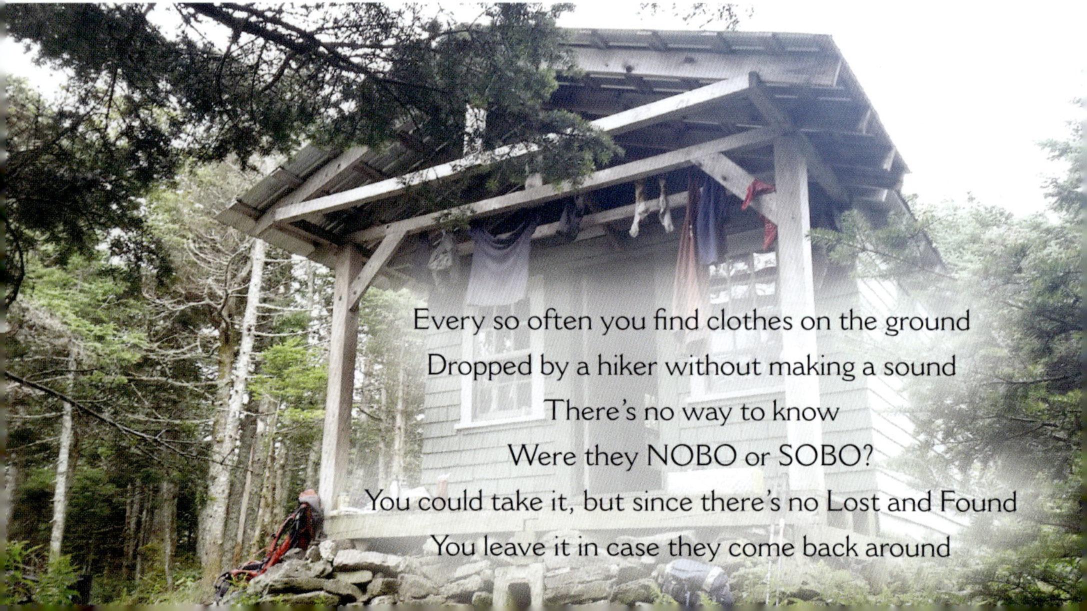

Every so often you find clothes on the ground
Dropped by a hiker without making a sound
There's no way to know
Were they NOBO or SOBO?
You could take it, but since there's no Lost and Found
You leave it in case they come back around

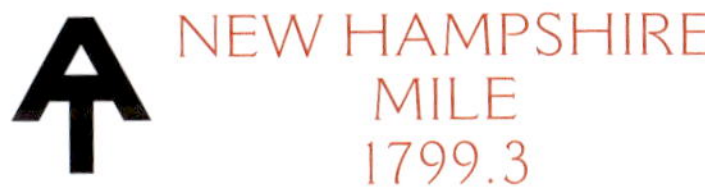

NEW HAMPSHIRE MILE 1799.3

Steepness redefined
When up is faster than down
Passage through tree line
Need hands equally as feet
Shiny spots show preferred path

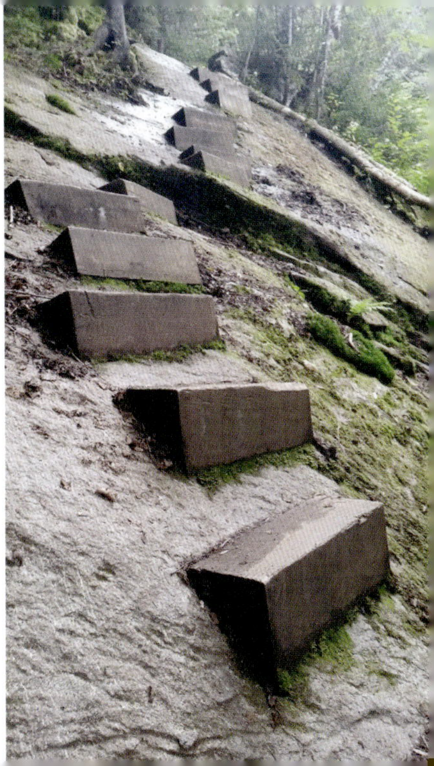

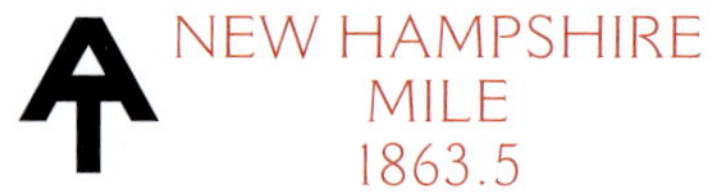

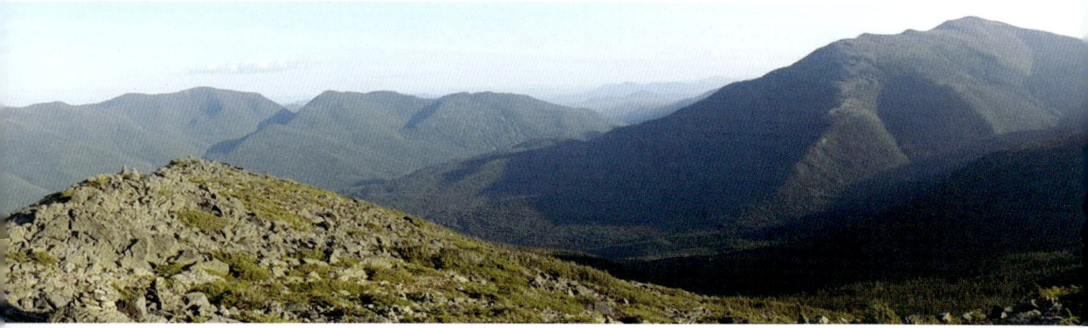

Presidential Range

Lichenless rocks between cairns

Alpine moonscape hike

View to prior days' summits

Glacial sculptures fade to white

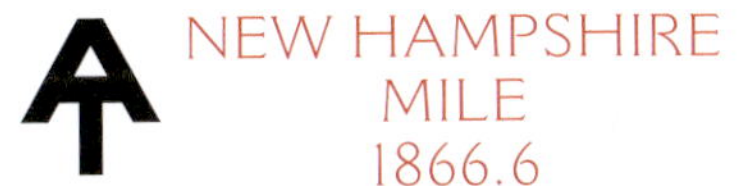

NEW HAMPSHIRE
MILE
1866.6

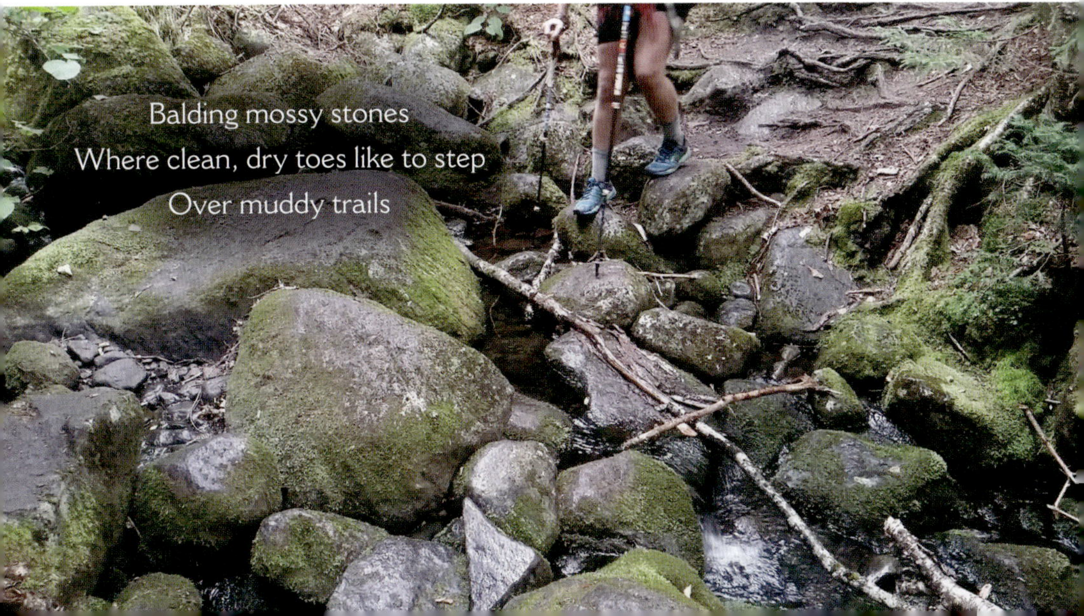

Balding mossy stones
Where clean, dry toes like to step
Over muddy trails

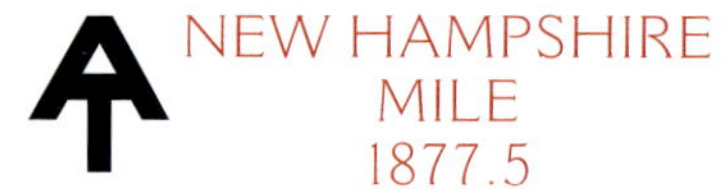

NEW HAMPSHIRE
MILE
1877.5

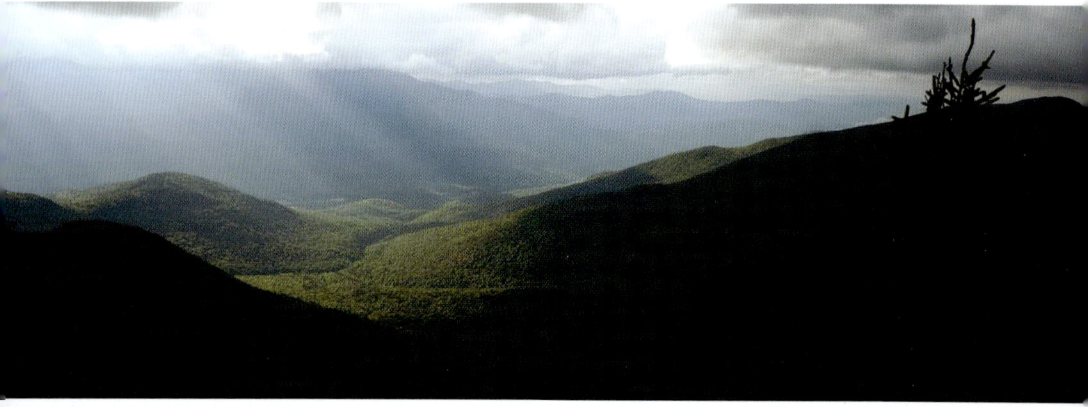

White Mountain speed bumps
Steep trails, rocks, roots, mud, tough lines
Views worth stopping for

NEW HAMPSHIRE MILE 1891.5

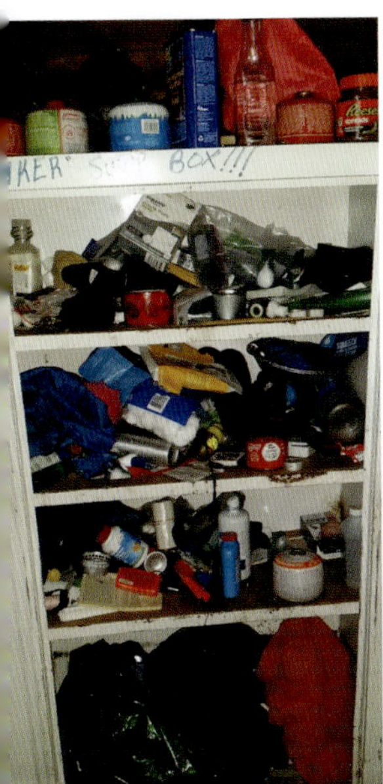

Before you resupply, play hiker box roulette
With expectations low, you won't be upset
When all you come to find
Is useless clothing left behind
Unlabeled bags of powder – vectors for disease
Fuel cans with enough liquid – equal to a sneeze
Dumpster diving glorified
Most others would be horrified
To sort through such a mess, feeling like a total sleaze

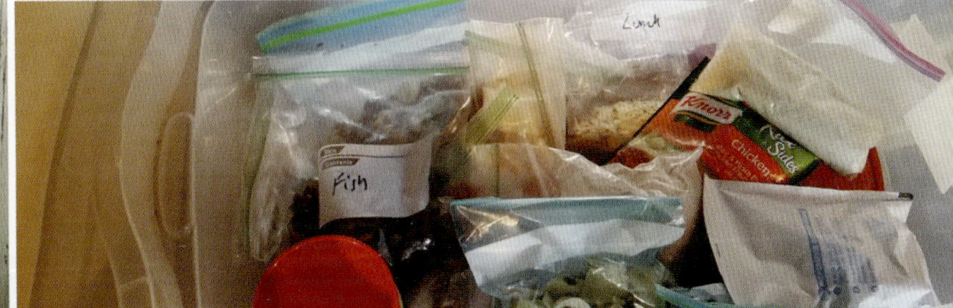

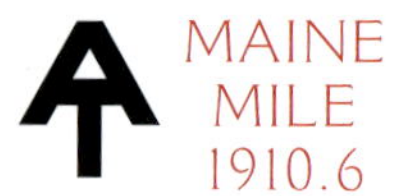

MAINE
MILE
1910.6

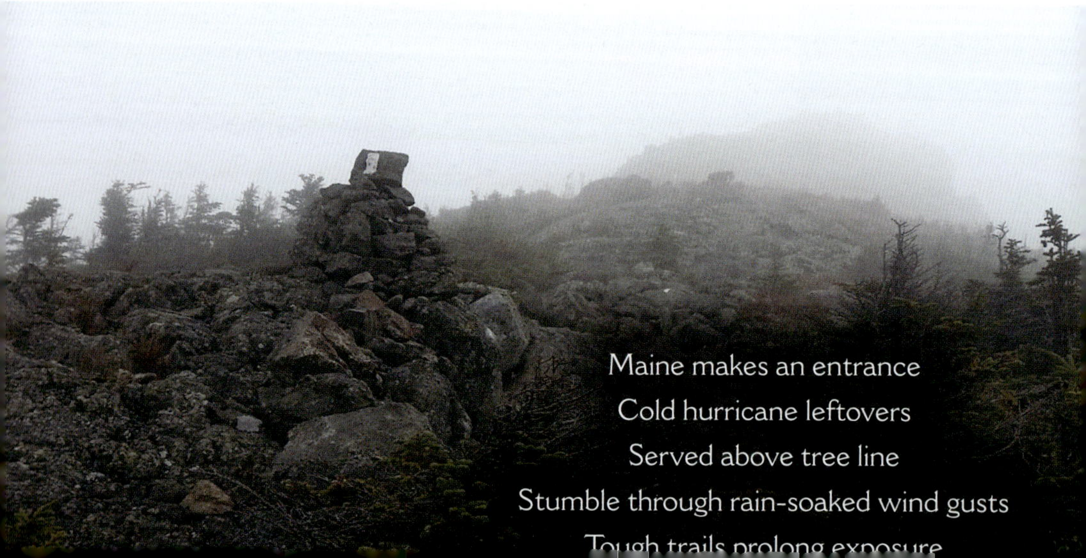

Maine makes an entrance
Cold hurricane leftovers
Served above tree line
Stumble through rain-soaked wind gusts
Tough trails prolong exposure

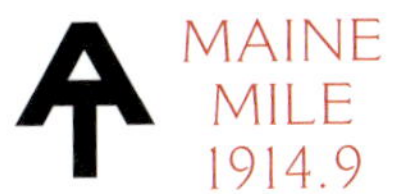

MAINE
MILE
1914.9

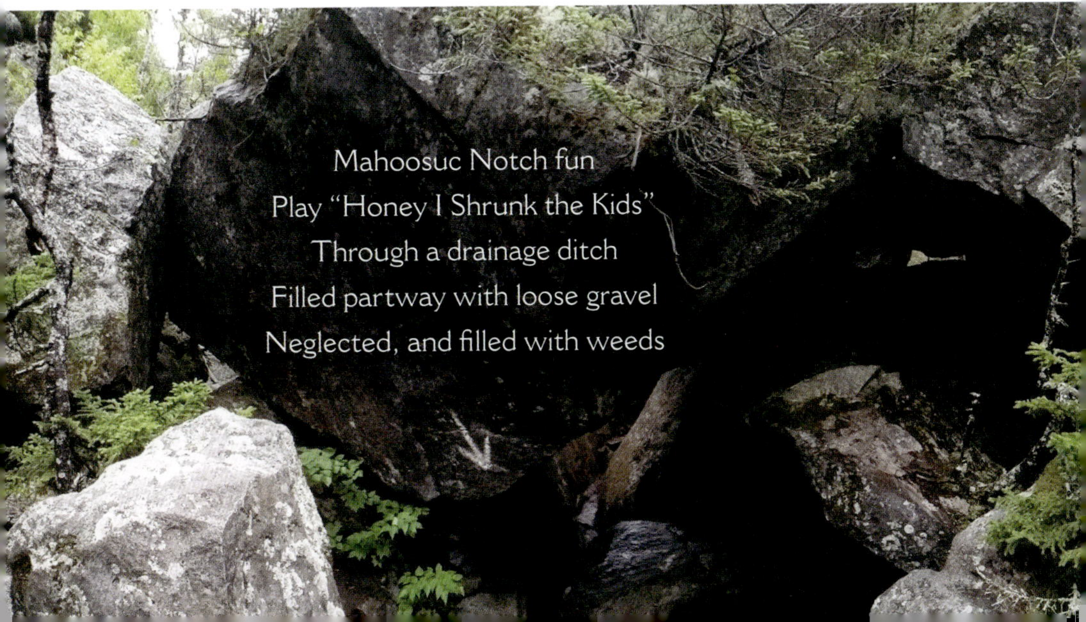

Mahoosuc Notch fun
Play "Honey I Shrunk the Kids"
Through a drainage ditch
Filled partway with loose gravel
Neglected, and filled with weeds

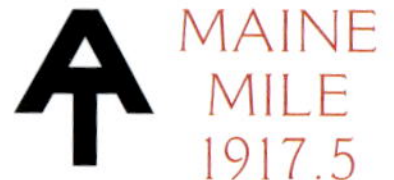

MAINE
MILE
1917.5

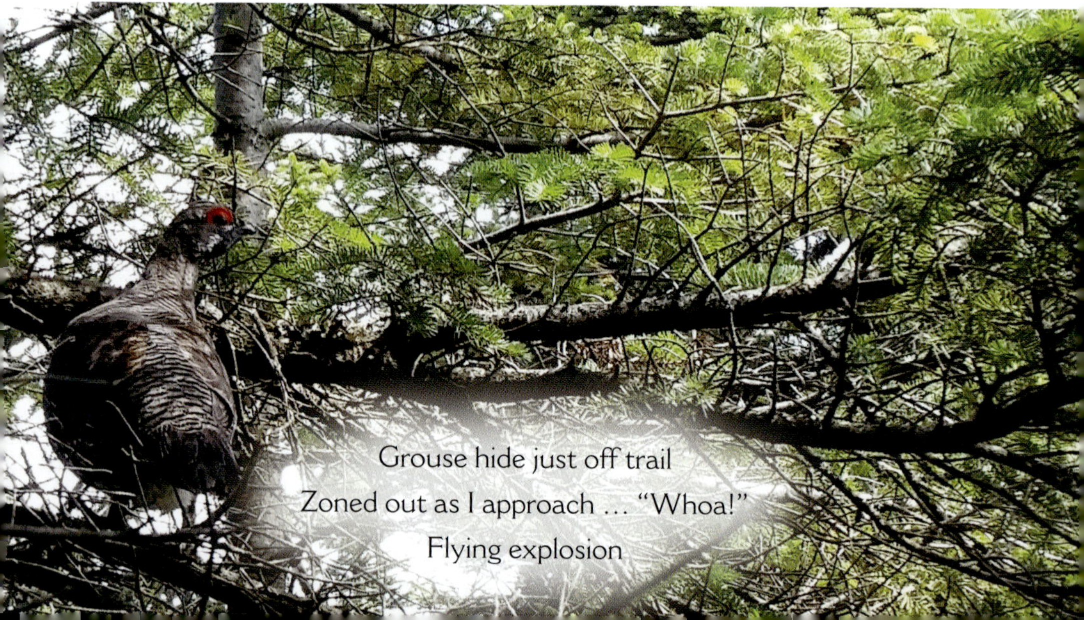

Grouse hide just off trail
Zoned out as I approach … "Whoa!"
Flying explosion

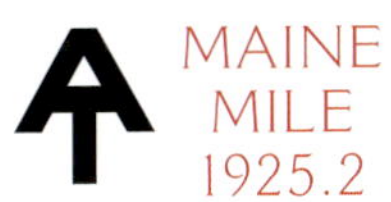

Raisin fingertips
The kind from bathtubs and pools
Or rain that won't quit

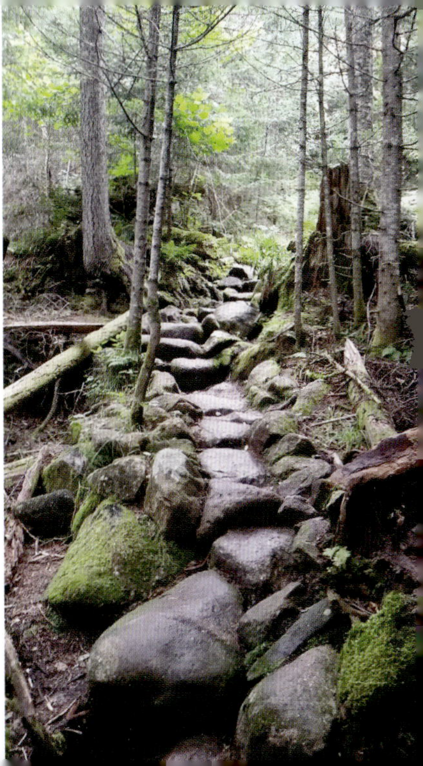

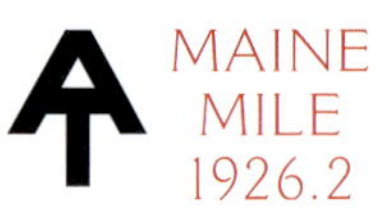

MAINE
MILE
1926.2

Why make a switchback
when you can build a staircase
Let's just go straight up

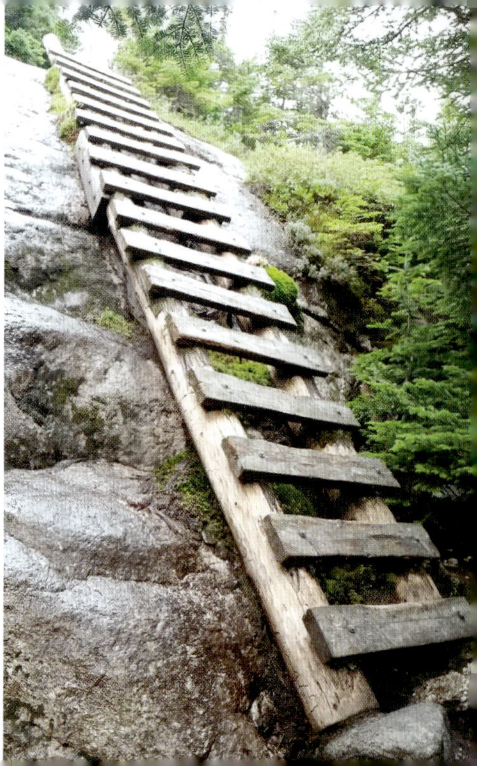

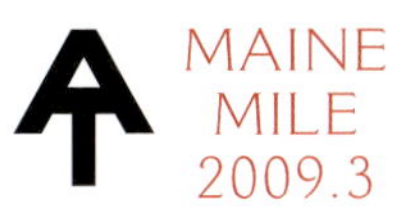

MAINE
MILE
2009.3

Sabbath Pond Lean-to
Soggy feet rest when rain won't
Loon-song lullaby

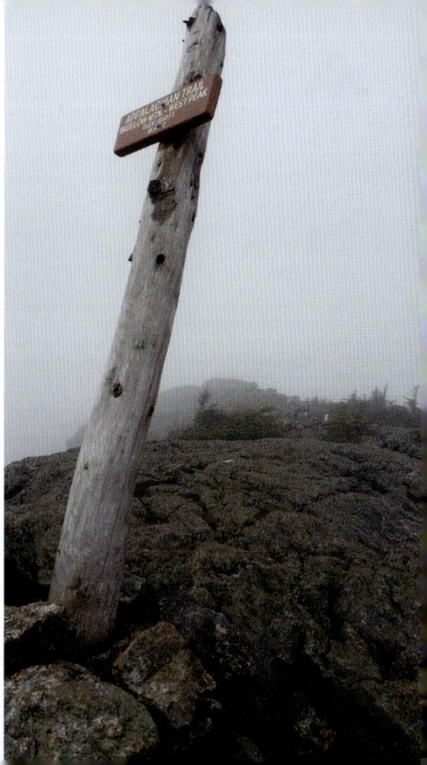

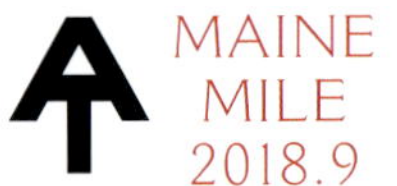

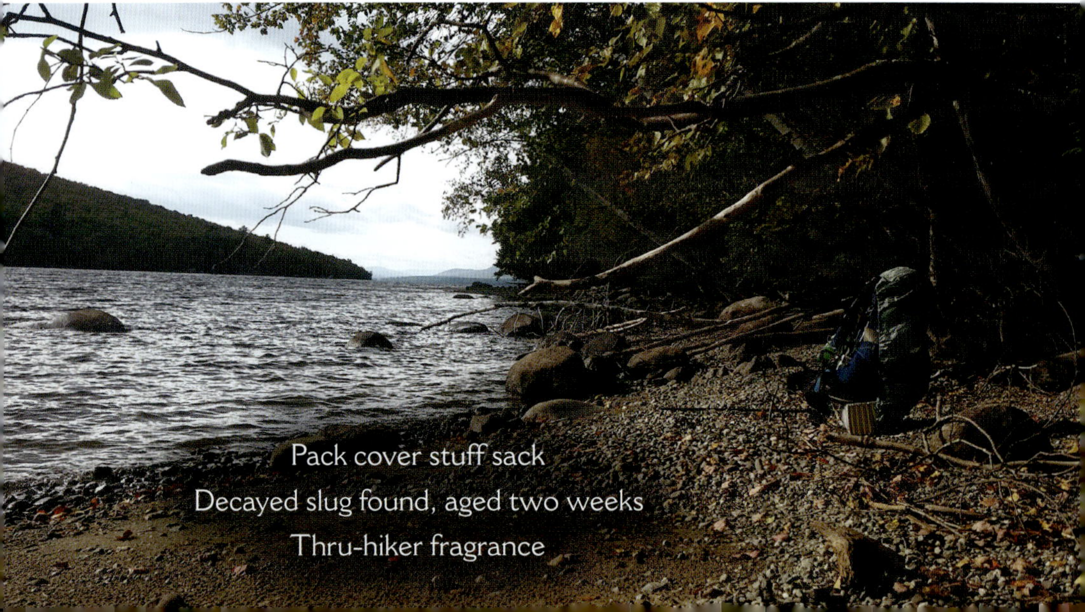

Pack cover stuff sack
Decayed slug found, aged two weeks
Thru-hiker fragrance

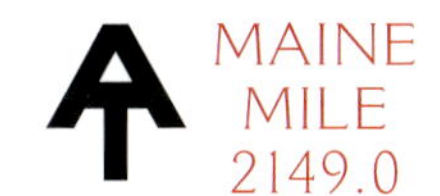

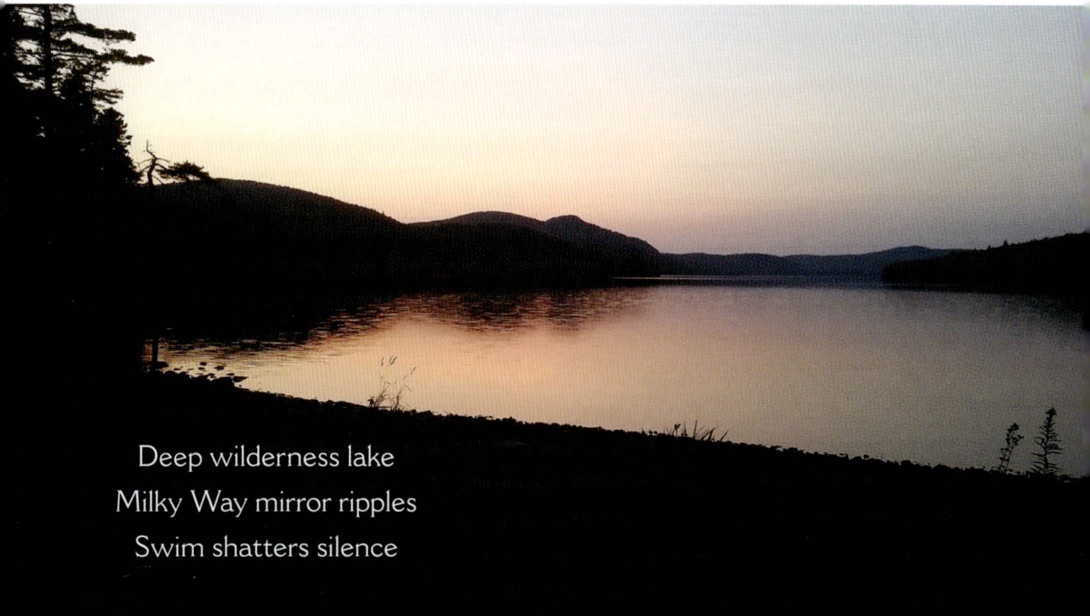

Deep wilderness lake
Milky Way mirror ripples
Swim shatters silence

MAINE
MILE
2159.7

Trail names are derived in multiple ways
Deprecating for some, while others give praise
Ask for the tale
Even if it's grown stale
It will help you recall after several long days
The matching name for a face during this unique phase
To reinvent expectation
For a new reputation
Not based solely on bullet points from long resumes
But on real interactions alongside the white blaze

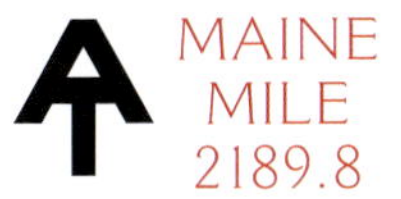

MAINE
MILE
2189.8

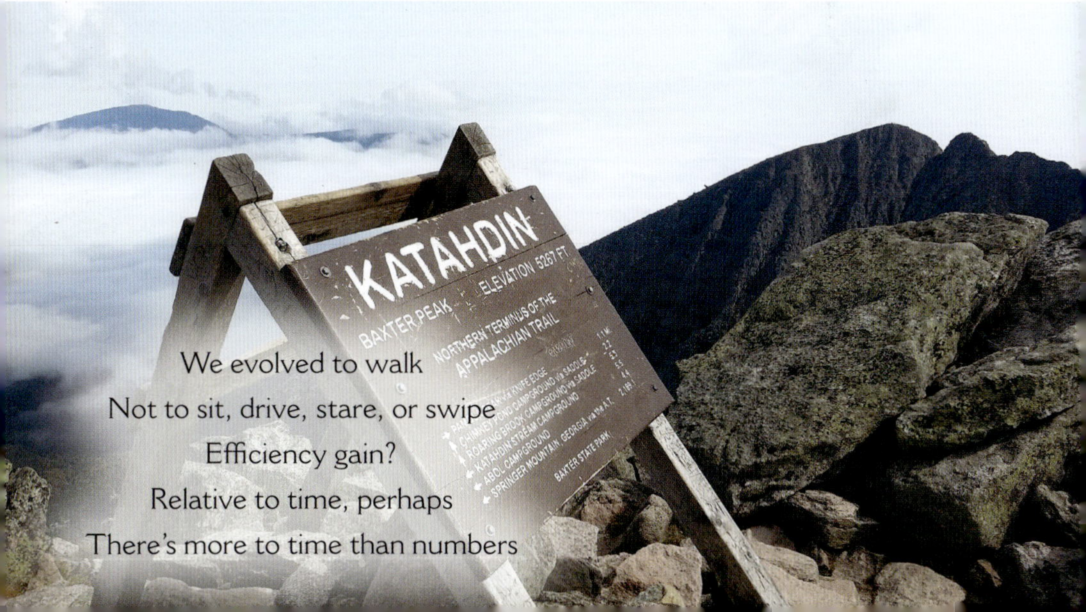

We evolved to walk
Not to sit, drive, stare, or swipe
Efficiency gain?
Relative to time, perhaps
There's more to time than numbers

I had difficulty matching the following poems with a corresponding photograph, but I believe they still effectively represent what many hikers experience on the A.T.:

Volunteers at work
Digging, clearing, trimming trails
Thank you for your time!

Who needs a hostel when there's plenty of creeks?
To jump in, have a swim, and wash laundry that reeks
A place to relax and dine
Make a backpack clothesline
At this rate I won't need a trail town for weeks

Fearful grasshoppers
Tickle an oak leaf carpet
Upon my approach

Trees growing on rocks
Topple over when windy
Scab of roots removed

City folk on Trail
Clean, well-groomed, no eye contact
Strong waft of fragrance
No response to my, "Hello"
Socially desensitized

Whack-a-mole surprise
Clear trail a moment ago
Just tripped on a root

Broken down hiker
Screech and General here to help!
Trekking pole busted
Super glue mistake...oh crap
Leatherman saw, duct tape... Fixed!

"That's a big, black dog!"
"Where's its owner?" I think...pause
It stops, glances, runs
A swift, peculiar gait...gone
This breed's not meant to be leashed

First one to make rounds
Walking through morning cobwebs
Songbirds gossiping
Critters run into hiding
Constable Screech on duty

Cold rain and strong winds push into the night
Along with shivering hikers, headlamps glowing bright
Hypothermic no doubt, as they roll into camp
Remove all their clothes, they're way beyond damp
There's no time to be modest
I'll be brutally honest
So put on dry layers with help from a spotter
Can somebody, please, boil some water?
With all hands on deck, her temp finally rose
Welcome to Maine, but stay on your toes!

Purple dots stain Trail
Mulberry tree hint...look up
Seeds stuck in my teeth

HUMAN-POWERED STATISTICS

Trail Miles[1]	2189.8
Bonus Miles[2]	41.9
Actual Miles[3]	2231.7
Total Calendar Days	141
Total Zero Days[4]	18
Total Hiking Days	123
Total Weeks	20.1
Trail Miles per Day, WITH Zero Days	15.5
Trail Miles per Day, WITHOUT Zero Days	17.8
Actual Miles per Day, WITH Zero Days	15.8
Actual Miles per Day, WITHOUT Zero Days	18.1
Total Lines of Poetry	633
Average Lines of Poetry per Day	4.5
Average Miles per Line of Poetry	3.5

1. Official length of the Appalachian Trail in 2017
2. Additional miles required for side trails to/from overlooks, water, campsites, resupply, etc.
3. Trail miles PLUS Bonus Miles
4. "Rest" days with zero trail miles

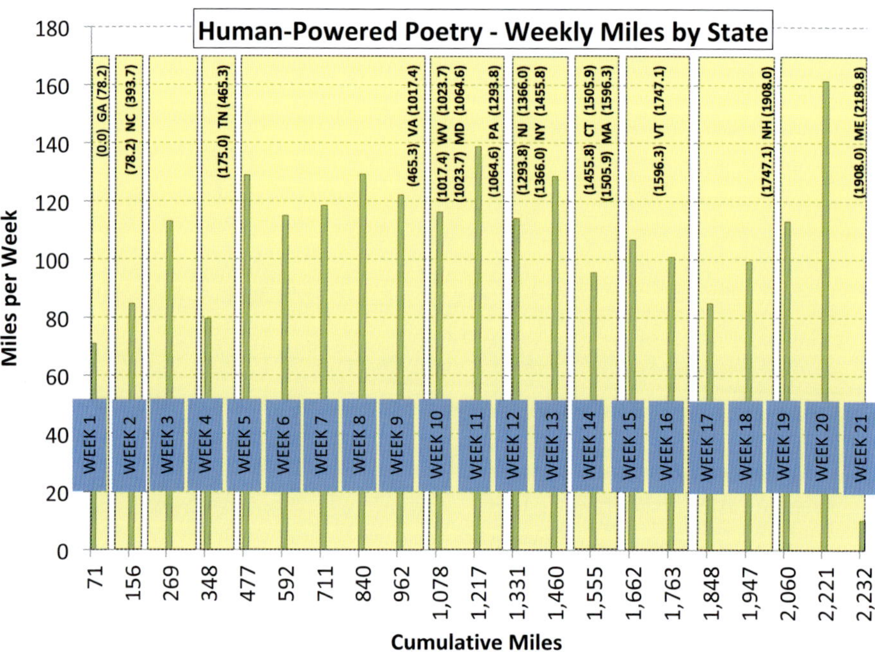

Human-Powered Poetry - Weekly Miles by State
Miles per Week
Cumulative Miles
180
160
140
120
100
80
60
40
20
0
(0.0) GA (78.2)
(78.2) NC (393.7)
(175.0) TN (465.3)
(465.3) VA (1017.4)
(1017.4) WV (1023.7)
(1023.7) MD (1064.6)
(1064.6) PA (1293.8)
(1293.8) NJ (1366.0)
(1366.0) NY (1455.8)
(1455.8) CT (1505.9)
(1505.9) MA (1596.3)
(1596.3) VT (1747.1)
(1747.1) NH (1908.0)
(1908.0) ME (2189.8)
WEEK 1
WEEK 2
WEEK 3
WEEK 4
WEEK 5
WEEK 6
WEEK 7
WEEK 8
WEEK 9
WEEK 10
WEEK 11
WEEK 12
WEEK 13
WEEK 14
WEEK 15
WEEK 16
WEEK 17
WEEK 18
WEEK 19
WEEK 20
WEEK 21
71
156
269
348
477
592
711
840
962
1,078
1,217
1,331
1,460
1,555
1,662
1,763
1,848
1,947
2,060
2,221
2,232

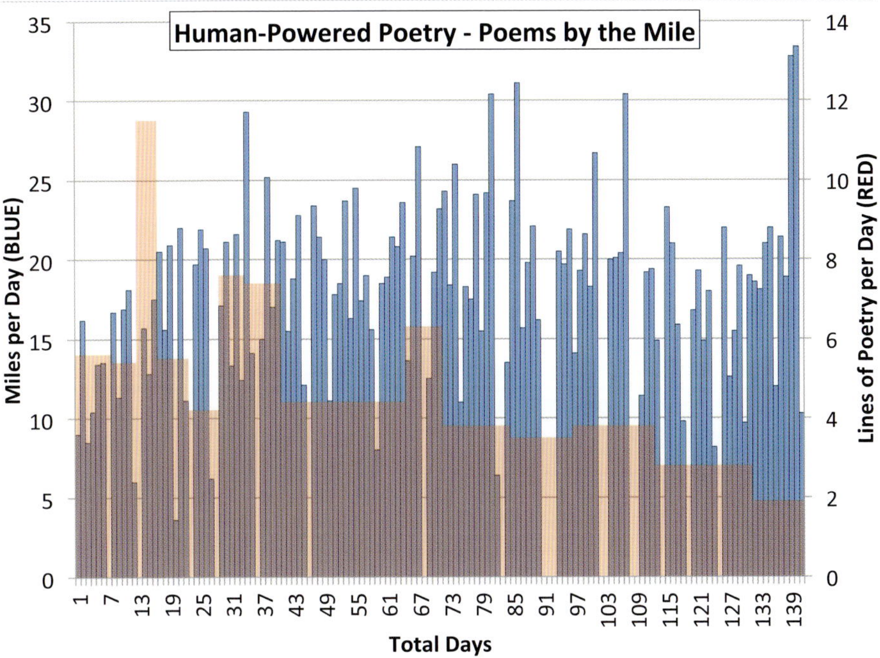

Human-Powered Poetry - Poems by the Mile
Miles per Day (BLUE)
Lines of Poetry per Day (RED)
Total Days
35
30
25
20
15
10
5
0
14
12
10
8
6
4
2
0
1
7
13
19
25
31
37
43
49
55
61
67
73
79
85
91
97
103
109
115
121
127
133
139

EQUIPMENT LIST

Room & Board

Silnylon Tarp
Bug bivy
Titanium Stakes (x16)
1.25mm Dyneema cord
(26ft, 16ft, 16ft)
P-cord
Hammock
Trekking poles
Sleeping bag (32°F)
Silk sleeping bag liner
Earplugs
SOL bivy
Z-lite Sleeping pad

Organization:

Osprey Exos 48L backpack
Bear bag kit
Small stuff sack
Small PLUS stuff sack (x2)
Small dry bag
Medium dry bag
Long slim dry bag
Wallet bag
Ziploc bags

Walk-in closet:

Wide-brim Hat
Light wool beanie
Fleece headband
Bug net
T-shirt, wool (x2)
Long-sleeve, wool (light)
Long-sleeve, wool (medium)
Long underwear, wool
Synthetic camp pants
Running shorts, Dri-fit (x2)
Running tights
Underwear (x2)
Running socks (x2)
Bedtime socks
Trail Running shoes
Sandals
Puffy jacket
Rain jacket
Rain pants
Thin gloves
Mitten rain shells

Bathroom:

Bodywash
Handkerchief (x2)
Toothpaste
Toothbrush
Floss
Body glide
Poop shovel
TP
Hand sanitizer
Goldbond powder

Office:

Map & Compass
Journal & pen
Wilderness permits

Kitchen:

Bamboo silverware
Gerber Knife
Jet boil PCS w/ fuel
Oil containers (x2)
Sawyer Squeeze water filter
  1L Platypus water bags (x2)
Water bottle w/ harness (x2)
Gatorade powder container

Utilities:

Smartphone w/ earbuds
Wall charger w/ cable
Goal Zero Flip 10 Battery
Black Diamond Headlamp
Maglight mini flashlight

Workshop:

First aid kit
Sewing kit
Bobby pin
Tenacious tape
Spare mini carbiners
Storm Matches
Cottonballs covered in vaseline
Spreadsheet with encrypted passwords
Wallet photocopies
Duct tape
Seam grip repair adhesive
Silnet repair adhesive w/ spare tarp material
Safety pins
Leatherman Wave Multitool

ABOUT THE AUTHOR

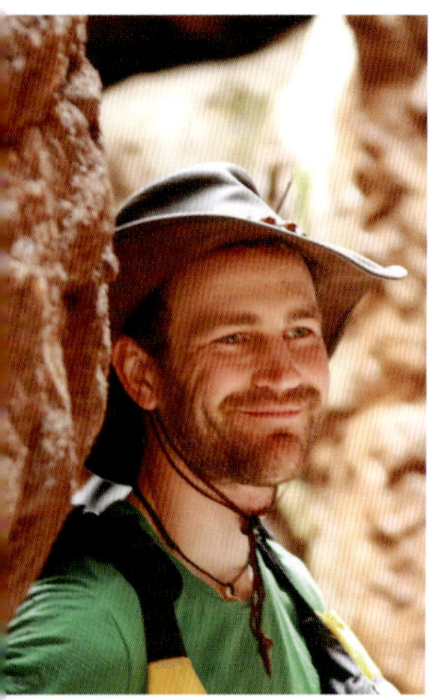

Photo credit: Alan Cammack, www.alancammackphotography.com

Daniel Zube is a professional mechanical engineer and inventor with a passion for improving the energy efficiency of various systems. He has published peer-reviewed, scientific journal articles in *Boiling Point*; *A Practitioner's Journal on Household Energy, Stoves and Poverty Reduction*, and also in *International Journal of Energy for a Clean Environment*.

Prior to his thru-hike, he had similar travel experiences including backpacking in Australia and New Zealand, cycle-touring through Europe, and rafting/kayaking through Grand Canyon National Park.

In his free time, you will find him planning his next adventure while engaging in various human-powered activities such as cycling, mountain biking, trail running, triathlon, and skiing. He is also a strong supporter of local organic agriculture and sustainable living practices.

Write your own poems here!

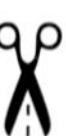

This page may be removed and recycled for an ultralight hiking experience.